BARRY DU BOIS

Barry Du Bois is an Australian designer, building expert and TV personality who is currently co-host on Channel TEN's Logie-award winning lifestyle program *The Living Room*.

He ran a successful design, building and property development business until retirement in 2005 and in 2011, hosted Network Ten's renovation reality series, *The Renovators* before joining lifestyle program *The Living Room* in 2012, alongside Amanda Keller, Dr Chris Brown and Miguel Maestre, as well as fronting *The Renovation King*.

Du Bois works tirelessly for many charities and is a member of the Board of R U OK? Day. He is also a passionate advocate for Cancer Council Australia and a firm believer in environmental sustainability.

He is married to Leonie and is the father to twins, a son and a daughter, born in 2012. He was diagnosed with plasmacytoma, a cancer of the immune system, in 2010 and underwent successful therapy, but in 2017 the cancer returned as multiple myeloma.

MIGUEL MAESTRE

Born in Murcia in the south of Spain, Miguel Maestre's passion for food and life is infectious, and he has developed a talent for incorporating Spanish ingredients and cooking styles into his Australian menus.

At 27 Miguel was head chef of Tony Bilson's Number One, working alongside Australia's leading French chef Manu Feildel. After meeting Ferran Adrià at the number one restaurant in the world, El Bulli, Miguel opened El Toro Loco at Sydney's Manly Beach, the biggest Spanish restaurant in Australia, when he was only twenty-eight years old.

Miguel has been awarded the highest award a citizen can receive by His Majesty the King of Spain, the Order of Civil Merit, for his extraordinary service to the nation for the benefit of Spain in the biggest retail distributor of quality Australian media. Miguel is in love with live cookery demonstrations and is by far the busiest chef on stage in the country, touring Australia to share his Spanish heritage and love for wholesome, tasty food.

It is Miguel's co-hosting role on Network Ten's three-time Logie winning show *The Living Room* that has catapulted him into the world of TV, working alongside Amanda Keller, Dr Chris Brown and Barry Du Bois. Other TV credits include *Boys Weekend* (airing in more than 100 countries worldwide, along with fellow international chefs Gary Mehigan, Adrian Richardson and Manu Feildel), *Miguel's Tropical Kitchen*, *Miguel's Feasts* and *Weekend Feast*, also airing on Network Ten.

Miguel is the author of two Spanish books, *Miguel's Tapas and Spanish Cooking*, and is the founder and owner of *Maestre Family Food*, the biggest retail distributor of gourmet Spanish products throughout Australia.

He also works very closely with Cancer Council Australia, OzHarvest and CARE Australia. He is the Australian Mushrooms Ambassador, representing the country's mushroom farmers and inspiring Aussies to make the most of our third largest crop.

BARRY DU BOIS AND **MIGUEL MAESTRE**

LIFE FORCE

AN UNFORGETTABLE STORY OF FAMILY, FRIENDSHIP, FOOD AND CANCER

echo

A division of Bonnier Publishing Australia
534 Church Street, Richmond
Victoria Australia 3121
www.echopublishing.com.au

Copyright © Barry Du Bois and Miguel Maestre 2018

All rights reserved. Echo thanks you for buying an authorised edition of this book. In doing so, you are supporting writers and enabling Echo to publish more books and foster new talent. Thank you for complying with copyright laws by not using any part of this book without our prior written permission, including reproducing, storing in a retrieval system, transmitting in any form or by any means, electronic, mechanical, photocopying, recording, scanning or distributing.

First published 2018
Reprinted 2018 (three times)

Printed in Australia.

> This book is not intended as a subtitute for medical advice or treatment. Any person with a condition requiring medical attention should consult a qualified medical practitioner or suitable therapist.

Cover design by Alissa Dinallo and Andy Warren
Principal photography: Sue Stubbs
Page design: Alissa Dinallo and Andy Warren
Typesetter: Andy Warren
Typeset in: Baskerville 10/14pt

A catalogue entry for this book is available from the National Library of Australia

ISBN: 9781760682996 (paperback)
ISBN: 9781760685560 (ebook)
ISBN: 9781760685577 (mobi)

bonnierpubau
bonnierpublishingau
bonnierpublishingau

www.mylifehouse.org.au

BARRY'S DEDICATION

This book was created because I wanted to share the dark and beautiful times in my life. But to do that, I needed the support of the strongest person in this world, the woman who has supported me, nurtured me, loved me without condition and whose dedication, belief and tenacity brought our beautiful children, Bennett and Arabella, into the world.

To my dear wife Leonie, my saving grace, my angel, my friend, my love, I dedicate this book to you.

MIGUEL'S DEDICATION

Cancer affects us all in some way. You might be battling the disease yourself, or have a friend, family member or neighbour who has been affected. I'm dedicating this book to my dearest friend Baz, whom I love very much. Baz has shown me that friendship is one of the biggest treasures in the world.

I also dedicate this book to the memory of my beautiful friend Stephane, who lost his battle with cancer a few years ago. It's been a long time without you my friend, and I'll tell you all about it when I see you again.

I also hope this book gives everyone who needs a little inspiration in their darkest moments help to find the light at the end of the tunnel. This is a book about friendship with a delicious happy ending. At the end of the day, all I know about is cooking and I also know that LOVE IS THE BEST INGREDIENT IN LIFE, AND EVERYTHING TASTES BETTER WITH IT IN IT.

Photo credits

Photo in Chapter 13 of Amanda and Baz in hospital by Maria Michael

Living Room photos in Foreword and Chapter 1 by Stuart Bryce and Paul Lovelace

Shaved head portrait in Chapter 15, Baz's arm with tubes and fluids and machine in hospital both Chapter 17, by Steven Chee

Photo of Barry at the beginning of Chapter 8, boat shot Chapter 9, newborn babies at the beginning of Chapter 11, hospital shot Chapter 11, from Barry's own collection.

All other photos including cover photography, by Sue Stubbs.

CONTENTS

Foreword by Amanda Keller ix

PART ONE
1 Spinning Plates 3
2 A Little House on the Highway 10
3 A Lesson in Honesty 23
4 Dollar Wally's 29
5 The Invention that (Almost) Changed the World 35
6 Learning to Fly 45
7 Depression 53
8 Drifting with Fraser 63
9 The Hordern Pavilion Boat Show 1968–75 77
10 A Double Miracle 83
11 My First Cancer 97
12 A Man's Gotta Sing 115
13 My Second Cancer 123
14 Spinning Blood 131
15 The Night Before Christmas 136
16 The Effect of Mindful Meditation 141
17 The Big Hit 146
18 Humanity 153

PART TWO
Nourish Your Body and Soul by Miguel Maestre 161
A Holistic Approach by Dr Judith Lacey 165
The Simplest Joys by Merran Findlay 169
Cooking for Baz 175
Acknowledgements 219

FOREWORD
BY AMANDA KELLER

'Long story short …' This is how Barry Du Bois begins nearly every sentence. It's become a running joke. Our heads roll back in mock slumber, we tell him to hitchhike to the end of the tale, we suddenly remember we've left the gas on in an adjoining country. I once pretended I'd been bitten by a tsetse fly – to great effect, mind you. But truth be told (there's another of his phrases), there is no better storyteller than Barry, and what a swag of stories he has to tell.

'When I was a builder/yoga instructor/tennis coach/ski instructor/aerobics instructor/mountaineering guide/Greco-Roman wrestling champ …' 'When I was at a Hollywood party with Drew Barrymore/When I predicted the Wall Street crash …'

The worst thing is, it's all true! He truly is the most remarkable man, and he's lived a thousand lives.

I distinctly remember the first time I met Baz. We were at a TV event – he was part of *The Renovators* on Channel Ten. His aura (and I don't normally go in for this stuff) just glowed. In a room full of TV people, he positively reeked of humanity and depth. We sonared each other like dolphins and knew instantly we were soul buddies.

By the time TV came calling for Barry, he'd turned his back on his life as a succesful property designer/developer (wouldn't we all love that sentence written about us) and was on a search for meaning. He infuses all he sees and does with this world view, whether it's work, family or charity. In the midst of dealing with his latest medical challenge, he took time to design and overhaul the volunteers' room at the Sydney Children's Hospital.

I know I make him sound like some kind of superhero (and who needs a cape when you have that hair?). But he bloody well is!

This is a guy who 'gives out', and that's what this book is about.

The Living Room is more than a TV show to its hosts. Barry, Miguel, Chris and I are joined at the hip. When one of us is hurt, we all bleed. Like our beautiful viewers, we are all on this journey with Barry. Dr Chris offered to take Barry's temperature. Strangely, Barry declined. I've asked to write this foreword. Barry wanted the woman who wrote *Fifty Shades of Grey* to do it, but I insisted. However, the friend who could be most useful at this time was our wonderful Spanish chef, Miguel.

Even without his delicious, soulful, life-affirming recipes, this man's personality would be enough to raise you from your sick bed. Sure, you might be leaping out of bed to stop him mangling the English language, or to stop him hogging the microphone at karaoke, but either way, his positive skew on life is infectious.

These two buddies are about to take you on a journey. If anyone can help us laugh though tough times, and accept change and new challenges by focusing on what matters most, it's these inspiring guys.

Happy reading. Happy eating. Happy living.

AMANDA

BARRY DU BOIS & MIGUEL MAESTRE

PART ONE

1
SPINNING PLATES

Why does this book exist?

Why am I sitting here writing at ten a.m. on a cloudless mid-spring day in Bondi? Why aren't I learning my lines for next week's show? Or working on a new building? Creating a new design? Going for a surf? A few birds are looping my joint a few blocks from the beach and the kids are running through the house. I can smell my wife Leonie's nutritious cooking.

Life's pretty perfect, you'd think.

Well, it ain't so great.

Last night on *The Living Room*, the Channel Ten show I'm on with my good friends Amanda Keller, Chris Brown and Miguel Maestre, I announced, to tears all around, that the cancer I'd been hit with six years ago was back.

It's back and it's aggressive.

I was shocked when the doctor told me. I didn't believe it when he told me six years ago and I didn't believe it this time. I was about to take Leonie and the kids to Turkey for a month on our yacht. I negotiated with my doctor to let me take the trip. It'd been a big year. I was tired. I wanted to relax.

And what if it was my last-ever holiday with the kids?

I was really scared for the first time in my life. An immense fear washed over me. Everything was different now. I had kids. I'm not nearly ready to go. I want to see my children's children and I want to nurture my kids all the way until adulthood.

I was angry, too. I blamed a lot of people and a lot of external forces. I blamed the medical industry. I blamed mobile phones. I blamed everything and everybody.

I quickly realised I couldn't just point my finger. I needed to get back to my normal way of thinking, which is: make the most of a bad situation. What could I do better? Straightaway I realised that I hadn't been eating well. I hadn't stretched. I was overworking. I wasn't exercising. I had to get back to the routine that had kept me healthy for six years.

Within seconds of my announcement going to air, amazingly … amazingly … thousands of messages of support started flooding in. It floored me how much people cared.

What concerned me, however, was that my message might become misconstrued as My Cancer Battle, a story about me.

It's not. I want everyone to know that I feel like I'm the luckiest bloke alive.

I have means. I live in the eastern suburbs of Sydney. I'm ten minutes from the best hospitals in the country and I've got incredible support around me.

I want to use this bad situation to inspire people. To help others lead a better life so they're less likely to get cancer or to be better prepared if it does come.

I always say that life is about spinning plates. Everybody says how difficult life is but it's difficult if you're trying to spin stacks of plates: work, kids, money, mortgage and so on.

The trick to life is to put everything that is required for a whole life on one plate – one well-balanced plate with the right proportions of everything you need on it: health, family, love, security, money etc. Then we'd all do okay. I'm happy with who I am. But there have been times when I've overanalysed things, when I've gotten incredibly frustrated over situations I couldn't control.

From 2000 through to 2008, I drifted in and out of depression. I was trying to control everything, to spin not just my plates but everyone else's as well.

Everything that has happened since my diagnosis has had a major impact on the way I think. I realised I have to make the most of what I've got right now and not layer it with other problems.

With my latest treatment, I struggle sometimes. I'm taking massive amounts of steroids, making it hard to sleep. It will be three in the morning and I'll be thinking, 'I'm not going to be able to get through the day, I won't be able to get through the script read, I'll look tired on the telly.'

My meditation teacher has taught me that that's a layer you don't need in your life. He teaches me that if I am awake at two or three in the morning, to make the most of that moment. It's up to me, to us, not to layer it with those negative optional extras. You don't need them and there's no need to take them on.

I've been an ambassador for the Cancer Council for five years and because I tell the story of my previous cancer, I know people get inspiration from that.

I've told my story of depression as part of R U OK and people give me feedback that they've taken support from it.

That's why I want to use this platform to help others. I don't need help. I don't. I'm happy to say that. I've got more help and support than anyone could understand.

But let's help people rally around others in need. And help people with cancer become aware of all the different treatments that are out there. When my mum got cancer, it was just a conveyor belt to the grave. The attitude from the establishment was, 'We'll give you drugs until you die.'

There was no consideration that she'd be healed; only that she'd die.

The holistic care that I'm receiving now, combined with the science and the knowledge we have from the medical profession, is there for people who live in big capital cities. There aren't 'Wellness Centres' in Lithgow or Nowra, or

Goulbourn where Mum died. There's a drug dispensary and palliative care.

I tell everybody that I talk to that cancer is not a foreign body. It's not something that infects us. It's not a disease that comes from the outside.

We're made up of millions of cells and they contain our DNA and everything about us. They're perfect. They're us.

Cancer is when something happens to some of those cells mutating to behave in an uncontrolled manner. To our immune system these mutated cells manage to hide so our body doesn't recognise them as a bad thing. In my case, the cancer is actually developed from some of these immune cells which is pretty crazy, and produce a protein which is used to track the activity of the cancer cells.

It's like the poo of cancer. The shit of cancer.

Now, if you exercise, reduce stress, if you have a good healthy balanced diet, well, it can help your immune system stay in good shape. And, as we learn more and get a better understanding of cancer and the role our immune system plays in combating it, we are becoming more aware of the impact our lifestyles and the way we treat our bodies may have. All of these activities and lifestyle changes can contribute to improving our immune system, and they can really help people getting through cancer treatments, keeping them resilient in both mind and body. How we treat our bodies may even help in reducing our risk of developing some cancers, reducing the risk of some cancers coming back after treatment. But there is still so much we still just don't know.

For many cancers, chemo is the medicine for that disease. What that actually means is this: you've got more good cells than bad cells but the bad cells need to be killed off. So they put chemo into your body to target those bad cells and some of your good, your healthy cells, particularly those that turn over quickly like your hair, the lining of your gut and some of your blood cells get knocked around too. So this can give the side effects from the chemo. It can make you feel lousy. But hopefully, you get better again.

When my mum passed away, that's how it was. Pump chemo in until finally it all caught up and she lay there gasping for air.

That's not going to be the case for me.

It's amazing what our body will do for us if we look after it. That's one of the messages of this book. I've been working with the people from the supportive care and integrative oncology team at Chris O'Brien Lifehouse Comprehensive Cancer Hospital and they've taught me that to effectively fight cancer you need to be in good shape both in body and mind. Perhaps this may help maintain a stronger immune system. I've learned that there are ways to keep well while going through cancer treatment. Taking control and learning to nurture yourself and knowing the tools out there that sit well with you to help keep you well during the journey with cancer can make it all much easier. It can make chemo easier, make the fight easier and hopefully can make the bounce back, the recovery easier.

We need a whole life. Not just eat shit, do what you want, get cancer and then fix it up with drugs or sit back and decide that you're going to die.

In Sydney, in a lot of big cities in Australia, there's way too much stress. When I came back from our trip on the boat, I said to Leonie, 'I haven't had any goodness since I've been back. I haven't had time to have sun on my skin. I haven't just pulled up a milk crate and talked to someone. I haven't had fresh food bought from a market and cooked outdoors.'

All of this has made me question it all. Why do one in three people have cancer now and fifty years ago that wasn't the case? Why are cancer rates higher in Australia and America than in Europe? Europeans smoke more. They drink more. Is it food? Is it the pressure of a high mortgage and long work hours? We're supposed to be advanced yet perhaps we're going backwards. We need to self-check ourselves because you can't rely on anyone else.

Depression came from me trying to spin too many plates. All that confidence I had allowed me to believe I could do it. It creates an imbalance. You've got to self-check and to self-balance.

As a society, we don't do these checks any more. There was a time when, by law, you weren't allowed to borrow money for a house if the payments took more than a quarter of your income. Society checked us. Now we have governments that aren't interested in humans, they're interested in business.

I can't spin those endless plates any more. I ran for local politics. I wanted to change the world. Those days are over.

On my plate now is my family, and they're surrounded by love, belonging, security, good food, touch, integrity and honesty.

That's the one plate I'm spinning and it's all I'm interested in spinning.

I hope you enjoy my book.

2
A LITTLE HOUSE ON THE HIGHWAY

I grew up in a two-bedroom fibro house that was full of asbestos, with a tin roof and a lean-to out the back on a six-lane highway. Fifty-seven Newbridge Road, Moorebank, Sydney. Right there in the middle of a flood zone, next to Bankstown airport and the Milperra Bridge.

Mum and Dad had bought it in 1960 for 1200 pounds after renting it for a year while they saved up the deposit.

It was a huge parcel of land with vacant blocks on either side. When I was a little kid, we were surrounded by hundreds of acres of bush which were later turned into an olive grove. Beautiful, beautiful soil.

My parents were the modern frontier people. Like so many others, they went out to the suburbs to build a good life for their family.

Our belief as kids, and as a family, was this: if we worked hard, if we were frugal and saved, good things would have to follow. We didn't have much but

Mum and Dad instilled in us an incredible sense of self-belief. Dad honestly thought he had the greatest family on earth. He used to say to us, 'You're a Du Bois, you can do anything.'

And we would have a school carnival or a project and he would say, 'You will be the best because you're a Du Bois.' And it wasn't until I was fourteen or fifteen that I actually realised he was just saying that. I really did think we were special. And it gave me this incredible confidence. If there was an athletics carnival, I was the fastest runner, and the highest and longest jumper. If there was anything physical you had to do, I would do it better. It didn't make sense that anyone could beat me at anything. I was the captain of the football team, captain of the soccer team, captain of everything. It was just accepted. Not because I was better. I definitely wasn't. We're all just bones and skin and blood but I believed it … I believed it … because of Dad. If someone asked me if I could do something, I'd say yes before they'd even finished asking the question.

Because I believed I could. Because of Dad.

Dad also believed that to do anything you just had to break it down into small pieces. He told me that any seemingly impossible big problem was just a bunch of little problems that could be solved. He pointed out to me when I was sixteen that my time for the hundred yards was only ten percent slower than the fastest person in the word. He told me, if you do everything you can, you can be ten percent better. And if you can't be ten percent better then be even one percent better.

It wasn't just running. It included building something, thinking about something, loving people, caring for people. He taught us never to stop analysing how we could do those things better. If you thought you'd done your best job, now your job was to do it a little bit better.

Our little house was modest compared to the three-bedroom joints with gardens that were populating the new estates around us. We didn't have a front yard because Dad always had something parked out the front he wanted to sell.

When Mum and Dad bought the house in 1960, the first thing they did was to spend the money on having it raised so it would avoid most of the water from the floods. We became obsessed with filling the raised area with soil so it looked like all the newer, more modern houses that sat on the ground.

Modern houses sat on the ground. That was the mantra.

Dad had a sign out the front, 'Top soil and clean fill wanted!' It never worked. All it did was create a big dam under the house.

But it was a great little joint.

You'd walk into the front room, which was a sun room, and to the left was a kitchen followed by the dining room. I use the word 'room' generously. It would've been three metres by three metres, tops. Off that was the bedroom I shared with my brother, Mick. Again, a little cell, three by three.

Back in the seventies, when we did most of our decorating, there were three types of wallpaper: the sunflowers, the European look and the ancient look. We had all three.

The kitchen was made of yellow Laminex, courtesy of my Uncle Pat, the carpenter, although nothing, and I mean nothing, not one single project, was finished. There was a stud wall that divided the kitchen and dining area. There was no Gyprock or fibro, just a tangle of electrical wires going through the frame. The kitchen cupboards were affixed directly to the studs at the top. Our 'splashback' was the view into the family room.

The lack of polish in our house wasn't because Dad was lazy. He just never had enough time for it. There were always other people to help. That was the ethos of my dad. He let my Uncle Pat, his younger brother, and Pat's wife, Auntie Jenny, live with us in a caravan in the backyard. Whenever Uncle Pat was short of work, Dad would say, 'Do a day's labour here and I'll pay ya.' Dad's opinion was you had to work every single day. If you didn't, it was ethically wrong. You had to work. You had to get up early and you had to go to work, whatever it was.

That was life, according to my dad.

Anyway, walk past the yellow kitchen and the stud wall and the wires and so on and you'd arrive at the lounge room where the TV was. Again, the room was three by three. We got a Rank Arena colour television in time for the Montreal Olympic Games in 1976. It was a huge expense to us. We bought the Rank Arena because Dad believed Germans did everything best. It was only timber veneer, but we saw it as a solid timber thing that would be with us for the rest of our lives.

Any consumer item that came into our house was a huge thing for us. We didn't get these things every week. This was our one purchase for the year. And the talk about buying a colour TV had been going on for the back half of 1975 and the first six months of 1976. Dad thought it was vitally important for us to see another country, in this case Canada, in colour. My dad hated credit but we had a payment plan. We put away a little cash every month until we paid it off and were able to pick it up.

I clearly remember the day Dad brought it home. We got it unpacked and it was sitting in its spot, pride of place. We turned it on and discovered we had the wrong aerial. My Uncle Barry, the sorta guy who'd be your techie today, quickly made a makeshift aerial and climbed up on the roof with it while Dad was in the living room winding the knobs and working the horizontal and vertical holds. Meanwhile, the kids sat there waiting for the miracle of colour. It was actually an anti-climax when it came alive because only a few of the programs were filmed in colour.

Still, we were very proud that we owned something we regarded as the best.

Over the years, we'd try little TVs around the house, black-and-white portable things so Mum could watch the news while she ironed, but neither Mum nor Dad liked TVs anywhere else. It's why I am who I am today, boisterous and confident, because we'd sit around the dinner table arguing points and not be comatose in front of the TV, even if the TV we had was a Rank Arena, German and, let's face it, pretty grand.

In our family debates, Dad would challenge us with why something couldn't be done and how we could make it happen. If you said something wasn't possible to my dad, it was like a carrot to a donkey. He would chase it forever. There was no such thing as 'can't' for Dad. We'd do everything from drawing on pieces of paper to balancing matchsticks or Paddle Pop sticks to prove our theories. Dad was a hands-on guy and he was very strong-willed. I can argue well but you couldn't argue with him because he would get louder and louder and gesticulate wildly. We would listen to Dad tell us about some goose at work and how, in his opinion, he was this and he was that, but you couldn't question it. He was the leader of the family.

But when Mum said it was time to end the argument, maybe it had gotten too

LIFE FORCE

heated or it was late, that was it. She'd look at him, never angrily, but sternly, and say, 'We've had enough, Bob.'

And that's where it shut down.

Walk past the lounge room and you'd hit, very quickly, the living room. It was a windowless box because originally it would have been the back of the house but there was another lean-to tacked onto the back. We had lean-tos on the front and the back. The back was divided into two rooms with a makeshift wall.

My sister lived in one and my cousin from Yass, Raymond, who was my age, slept in the other. He came from Yass because there was no work in the country back then. Both of us had the option of being a carpenter or a mechanic. He chose mechanic and I chose carpenter, because they were our uncles' professions and we could get jobs with them.

And then you had Uncle Pat and Auntie Jenny in the backyard caravan.

We all shared our meals and there was always boisterous conversation. There were plenty of doors to slam, too, if you got the shits and needed to let off steam.

It was a tiny house but we could always find the room to fit in one more person.

People talk about their first memories. I truly believe mine is from my bassinet. I remember it so clearly. There's a beautiful big willow tree in the backyard and I can see my mum and her hair is up in a bun. She's wearing a floral dress with an apron over it and she's hanging clothes on a line that has two posts with cross-members and wires going between it. And she pulls one side down, props it, puts the clothes on it, and then she pushes the other end up and locks that in and hangs the clothes on the other.

I can feel the warmth on my face and the yellow wattle trees are behind us. I can hear the humming of the insects. There's no garage in the backyard, no other structures.

Later, when I spoke to Mum and Dad about it, they told me I could only have seen that if I was younger than eighteen months because shortly after buying the house in late 1961 Dad bought a Hills Hoist from an auction. Mum hated the old line with the two posts and thought it was dangerous.

Now, can I remember that?

How did I know about the old washing line?

It's an episodic memory that flies in the face, really, of studies that show two years is the limit of our memories before childhood amnesia kicks in.

But I remember it. I know it happened. Mum. The dress. The old washing line. The insects.

Even now, I can close my eyes and feel the warmth of the spring sun on my face.

———

A great thing about living out west was the arrival of Gypsies, which happened once or twice a year. They'd always come in the night in their horse-drawn wagons and set up camp in the vacant land next to us.

We'd wake up and Dad would say, 'Don't go into the paddocks, the Gypsies are there.'

Now, I know it isn't politically correct to call Roma, many of whom had come from England or Greece, Gypsies, but back then, that's what we did. Dad would get changed, put on his I-mean-business-outfit of pants, shirt and shoes, and walk straight over there. I never knew what he talked about but he was there for fifteen minutes and then he'd come straight back and tell us how long they'd be staying for. He'd always warn us, 'Don't go onto that block. Stay away from 'em.' When they gave us stuff, he'd tell us not to take anything from them.

If I asked, 'Why did you go over there, Dad?' he'd tell me to mind my own business.

Years later, Uncle Baz told me Dad's welcoming speech would go like this: 'Bob Du Bois is my name. You're welcome to stay as long as you like. But I want to know when you're leaving. This is my boundary line. This is your line. Don't cross it. And don't go near the kids. If anything goes missing I'll cut your throat.

If you need a hand with anything just call out and I will help you. If you go the wrong way, this will go the wrong way. It's up to you.' And the chat would always end with a hand shake.

It wasn't Dad's land they were on but it was in our domain. It was our home. The speech summed Dad up. If you followed a few simple rules, everything was sweet.

Don't follow his rules and all hell would break loose.

I wish we were more like that now. I wish we had clearer boundaries and not the wishy-washy rules where no one really knows … exactly … what's right or wrong.

With my dad, there was a black and there was a white.

No greys.

———

My dad worked one job for wages but he always had a side bet, whether it was building box-trailers, reconditioning lawnmowers or raising poddy calves.

Every year, we'd go to the cattle auctions and buy two poddy calves for forty bucks apiece. We'd raise 'em in a little corral in the backyard and the following year we'd sell 'em for two hundred each.

When he came home from working all day, Dad would go into the shed and fold and weld box-trailers, which were very popular items in the sixties and seventies. Dad had made one that had a canopy over it so you could use it for camping. It was like what would become the trailer caravan. People went mad for 'em.

He'd build one for someone and then another person would swing by, say they wanted a certain length and he'd tell 'em it would be ready by the following weekend. He would work that fast. Twenty hours if he had to. He'd buy new axles and new springs and fit it all up overnight. The bloke would turn up and give him the cash.

Later in life, Dad saw that lawnmowers were going to be very popular. Our area had been surrounded by these new housing developments, all with little patches of grass front and back. Dad knew everybody would want a lawnmower so he started 'Moorebank Mowers'. And that became a booming business.

Dad had this little trick which I loved. On the sign, he had 'Moorebank Mowers' but he'd reversed the R even though he'd used a template for the letters.

Mum said to him after he'd put it up at the front of the house, 'You've buggered up the sign.'

He said, 'No, I've done it deliberately.'

Mum said, 'Why on earth would you do that?'

He said, 'Everyone thinks they're smarter than me so they'll come in to tell me I've buggered it up and I'll sell 'em a lawnmower.'

The amount of blokes that would come in and say, 'I don't want anything but I just want you to know you've buggered up that R, it should be the other way around,' then walked out with a lawnmower was insane.

Dad said, 'If a man thinks he's smarter than me, I guarantee I can sell him something. Because I'll just let him think he's smarter.'

We knew Dad's trick so when we saw a bloke pushing a new mower around we used to crack up. Dad had done it again! Whenever we saw someone looking at the sign and walk in, we would scream, 'Dad! Someone's here for a mower!'

Dad would walk down the stairs and as per the unwritten script the bloke would say, 'I'm not here to buy anything, mate, I'm here to tell you your sign's wrong.'

And, sure enough, half-an-hour later, Dad would be in the backyard testing it for the bloke. He guaranteed each mower would start with one pull and so Dad would pull the rope, it'd start, he'd tickle the carby up and then mow a portion of the lawn. Our lawn was only ever partially cut because Dad needed his patch of long grass to demonstrate the effectiveness and power of his lawnmowers.

A fully-reconditioned Victa lawnmower was about forty dollars back then. As the bloke was leaving, Dad would say, 'I don't have a catcher but if you come back in a week I'll have one for ya.' And he'd go to the auction, buy it for a dollar, rub all the rust off, repair it, and have it ready for him for another twelve bucks.

Dad could sell anything. He taught me everything I know.

The first time I saw my dad cry was when my brother got sick with a hernia. It's a story I always think about. Mick's a powerful man now but as a kid he was always sickly, and much smaller than me.

Mick was eleven when he got the lump in his groin and had to go in for surgery. It scared my dad. Because my dad was upset it frightened the hell out of me. How could this powerful man be so vulnerable?

And then he cried.

Seeing Dad cry terrified me at the time. It worried me because I suddenly wondered what could happen. Was it worse than we'd been told? Was Mick going to die?

On the upside, it happened in January right around my brother's birthday. Mick had always wanted a slug gun, an air rifle, and my dad said, 'Righto, son, I'll get you a slug gun.'

So here we are. It's 1972, which doesn't feel that long ago to be honest, and Dad and I are walking across the carpark at Bankstown hospital with a rifle in our hands.

Picture this. Dad sets up a wall of tin cans on the kerb and we catch the lift to my brother's ward where, ironically, the kid next to him is there because he was shot in the arse with a slug gun.

Mick's eyes light up when he sees the slug gun and Dad is happy because Mick is so happy. Dad says to him, 'Well, son, I've set some cans up for you for target practice. We should be able to hit 'em from the window.'

We're on the seventh floor, in a hospital ward, cranking a slug gun and firing at tins on the kerb. Dad shows Mick how to hold the slugs … lead slugs … in your mouth so they don't get dirty.

Dad shows Mick how to line up the sights and teaches him how to squeeze, and not pull, the trigger.

'Do that and you won't miss,' Dad tells Mick.

Ping! Ping! Ping! Mick is hitting everything.

A nurse walks in just as the kid with a slug in his arse and his dad are having a go.

'What's going on?' she says.

'We got my kid a slug gun for his birthday!' hoots Dad.

Soon, the nurse is shooting at the cans.

Then the matron walks in, furious.

Then she has a shot.

Even the doctor, who has a cigarette hanging out of his mouth 'cause everyone smoked back then, has a shot.

From my dad crying to all of us in tears of laughter.

It's a great moment in my life.

In 1988, a flood washed through Moorebank that was bigger than anything we'd ever experienced. Typically, whenever a flood was coming all of my close mates would come down from the suburbs, the new estates, and help get everything up onto the kitchen table. Usually, the water might rise to a foot or so within the house. There was no carpet, only lino, so once the water had receded, all it needed was a bit of a mop.

Floods had come through in 1969, 1975, 1976, 1978 and 1986. Nothing game changing but enough that we'd have to get everything up on the kitchen table and then we'd put all the other stuff on the box-trailer and take it up to the Milperra Bridge, the highest point around. Everyone in Moorebank would be there with all their stuff jammed into box-trailers, many of 'em made by my dad.

Back-to-back low pressure systems on April 30, 1988, however, caused the Georges River, one of the most flood-prone rivers in New South Wales, to burst its banks. One thousand houses were under water.

It was hard for my mum to get over it. As my brother and sister and I had become older all those unfinished jobs around the house started to get finished. Finally, Mum's house was completely finished.

Forget that, she already had a home.

What happened was that Mum started to get the niceties of life that she'd never had. I bought her a new lounge, we bought new TVs, all those consumer items. We were all working and doing well and Mum had done everything for us so it was a pleasure to help her. And, financially, with the kids gone and the house paid off, Mum and Dad weren't struggling like they used to. They had even gone on a cruise. Life was good.

And then came the Great Flood of 1988. All the normal precautions we took weren't enough. It was heartbreaking to see the things that meant so much to Mum disappear. The entire wall unit, her pride and joy which was filled with trinkets all carefully collected and curated, was ripped off the wall and washed out the door by the flood.

The next morning, I remember watching Mum in her nightie, the one thing she had left, trying to clean the house. She had nothing left. My mum never had anything, really, but those trinkets were everything to her.

We thought we'd get Mum and Dad back on track but what happened was that people started to ask for compensation from the government. My dad never once claimed any flood relief. He wasn't interested. It's not what we do.

But people did. And the government responded by forcing people who lived in 'high-risk' flood areas to accept compensation and to leave.

Dad had no intention of going. He said, 'This is our home. We'll raise it up another five feet if you like but we're not leaving. This is where my kids grew up, this is our home.'

And they said, 'Oh well, we'll give you a lot more than this is worth.'

Dad said, 'I don't care what you think it's worth, I'm not interested in selling.'

In the end, they gave us a price. There was no negotiation and it was about a hundred grand under what you could buy a house for in the area. It really buggered us up. Mum and Dad had a small amount of savings but what it meant was they had to go twenty k's out to Campbelltown, a small city that had none of those things Mum and Dad wanted. It didn't have a highway Dad could sell shit off. It didn't have space all around us.

They ended up in a secondhand, three-bedroom Masterton home. It was the suburbs. My dad hated it.

In hindsight, it was obvious a developer wanted that land for factories. And he'd lobbied the government with the line, you get me this, I'll raise it with fill, and I'll build my factories.

And that's what happened in several flood zones.

It happened in nearby Chipping Norton, too. That was once all vineyards. Then the developer came, got it, filled it fifteen feet, had it rezoned residential and created a housing estate.

Seeing my parents lose their house to a government buyback at the behest of a property developer was one of the reasons I feel resentment towards corporate Australia. As much as I love capitalism and how much money I've made out of it, I resent the fact that corporate Australia controls the government. Most people don't realise that. There are only a dozen or so people running this country.

And none of 'em are elected. You don't have a free market where the government controls the masses to make it work. What sort of society is that?

One thing the developer couldn't take or the floods wash away are the beautiful memories of a house filled with love and belonging.

Thirty years later, Mum and Dad had retired to a cottage near the beach down the New South Wales coast while Leonie and I were living in a penthouse in North Bondi. We always thought we'd raise any children we had there and we'd stay there forever, extending it if we had to.

One day Leonie came home with a brochure for a house in one of my favourite streets in South Bondi. It was a big old house with stained glass windows under a canopy of old trees in a cul de sac. A real grandma and grandpa house.

I had a profound thought. There are no old people in our lives and I wanted my children to have that same warm feeling 57 Newbridge Road gave me. I saw the footpath outside and I could imagine the kids running home from school with their backpacks.

When I turned up to inspect the house I felt it gave me a smile and a bit of a wink. It reached out to me and indicated it would be happy to protect, hold and love my family, and always welcome us with a smile.

A few months later, the penthouse was sold and Leonie and I moved in.

3
A LESSON IN HONESTY

Honesty, integrity and a ferocious work ethic were the key pillars for my dad. There was nothing more important to him. Get up in the morning and go to work. If you don't have work, find it. If you're in business, your personal integrity is your calling card. Pay your bills on time. Don't live beyond your means. If you don't have the cash, you can't buy it.

These aren't lessons you get from high school or university. They don't come as prepared lessons you can just warm up from reading books or attending conferences. These are priceless gifts that come from your parents and mentors. And I remember receiving all three of 'em on a hot December day in 1971.

I was eleven years old. We'd just bought a new Kingswood station wagon, a HT. I loved that car. I can even remember the numberplate, AYD 503. Mum and Dad had saved up the eighteen hundred dollars and we traded in our old one for the new Holden, and we proudly loaded it up for our annual six-week summer holiday to Easts Beach holiday park in Kiama, in the Illawarra region of New South Wales.

When I think about it, Mum and Dad would've budgeted for that holiday down to the last twenty cents. Mum and Dad's ethics meant you never borrowed money for a holiday. And there were no such things as credit cards in 1971. So every cent, for every day, was carefully accounted for. You didn't buy fun in those days; you made it. Each Friday during the holiday, with much ceremony, Dad would walk down to the shops, buy a Violet Crumble bar and divide it into four pieces, one for me, one for my brother Mick, one for my sister Liz and one for Dad. Mum never got a piece. That was her trying to be health conscious. We had tinned peas and mashed potato every night. To Mum, that was healthy.

Before we hit the highway, we called into the fruit and veggie shop, which was owned by a local Greek guy. We went there every day and Mum loved him. Dad didn't trust him. He was sceptical of every Eyetie (as we called Italians in those less enlightened days), every Greek, every Asian, not there were many of them, but he wasn't racist. He wasn't a bigot. You know the sort of bloke. He'd back an underdog with his own life. It was a different era.

Mum gave me five bucks to get a packet of Viscount cigarettes for her and Dad to smoke on the way, a packet of Fantales and a packet of Jubes for Dad. And the kids got a couple of pieces of fruit for the journey.

In those days, it took four-and-a-half hours to get to Easts Beach. From Moorebank we used to go out via Picton and over to Razorback mountain. It was a long drive and as we came over the hill and into Kiama, we'd always stop for fish and chips.

These were things we thought about all year. Isn't it a great way to live, where you can actually wait twelve months for something? There it was. A year's worth of anticipation to sit in a car with your family, the people you loved most in the world, obscured by cigarette smoke, with Mum reading out what it said on the Fantales wrapper and Dad always having first shot at answering the 'Who am I?'

As we pulled into the fish and chip shop, Mum asked me for the change from the fruit and veggie shop. I fished around in my shorts for a second and pulled out change from ten dollars.

Ten dollars? It didn't make sense. Mum had given me five. And ten dollars in those days was a lot of money.

Dad saw the money in Mum's hand.

'Where did that come from? Where did all that money come from?' he asked.

And, then, straightaway because Dad didn't have to think about these sorts of things in his head, didn't have to process the rights and wrongs to spit out the correct answer, he said, 'We have to go back. We have to go back right now.'

And I said, 'I didn't realise, Dad. I'm sorry.'

Dad looked at me, gravely but kindly, and said, 'It's not your fault, mate, but that man worked for that money. It's his money. It's his family's money. And I can't start a holiday knowing we've got it.'

So we closed the doors of the car, started the engine and drove the four-and-a-half hours back to Moorebank. Dad never talked about it again. It didn't matter to him. That man had worked for that money and so it had to be returned.

We drove home, stayed overnight, returned the money to the Greek man at the fruit and veggie shop first thing in the morning and then drove the four-and-a-half hours back, one day and one night late for the most precious holiday of our year.

I didn't realise it as an eleven-year-old boy but when I had children, the story came back to me. That's what counts. That's what makes you the man you are.

Look at me. I can barely read and write, had a bit of help getting the words on the page here I'll admit, and couldn't do much more than run fast and be decent in a stink.

I've done okay because I've stuck to the rules that Mum and Dad taught us. Mum never questioned the journey back. You've got to think of the time and the expense and the money driving back would've meant to their budget. We probably missed two or three Violet Crumbles over the course of the six weeks. Maybe we didn't get to go to the circus that was always in town over summer. Maybe we didn't get to share a slug each in the shooting gallery or get to throw a ball at the tins.

Not long after that, Ward 'Pally' Austin, who was a famous radio announcer in the sixties, sideswiped my dad in his car when he was drunk. Dad hated Pally because he spoke with an American accent even though he was born in Darlinghurst. Dad was the sort of bloke who sat there yelling abuse at the radio, first at Pally, and later at Alan Jones.

Dad just … hated … the bloke.

What are the chances Pally would crash into him?

But one night he woke us up at midnight to tell us what had happened, that Pally Austin was pissed and had crashed into him, and that it was best if we didn't tell anyone until tomorrow.

That was Dad. He didn't care who you were. It didn't matter whether he hated you or loved you. If you had a bit of bad luck, he'd help you out. Dad was always there with a hand to help a man back onto his feet. He had a titanic respect for every man, from the pauper to the king, until you proved him otherwise.

Dad didn't have many rules but he stuck by 'em.

What a man.

BARRY DU BOIS & MIGUEL MAESTRE

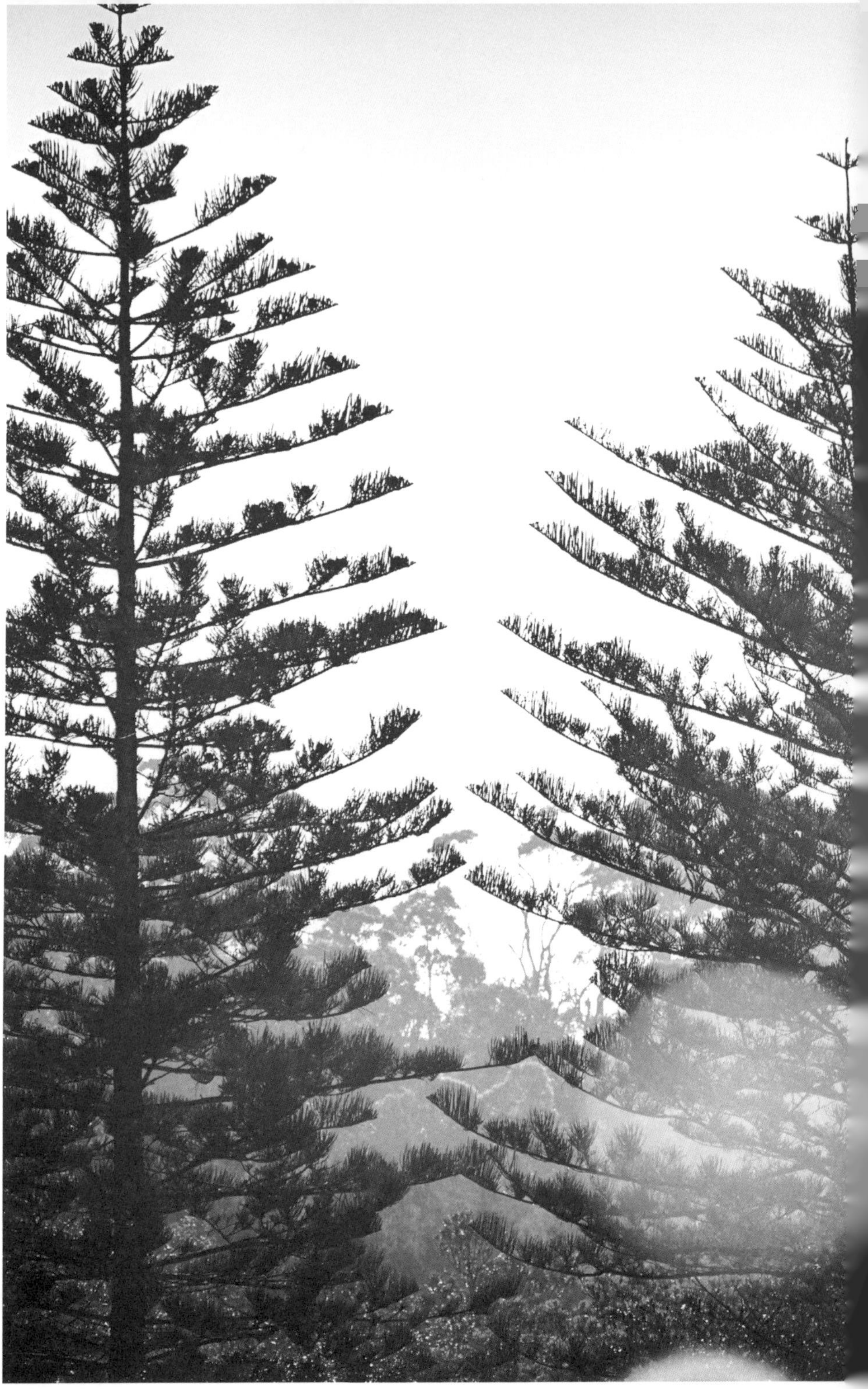

4
DOLLAR WALLY'S

Dollar Wally's was a wrecking yard on Riverside Road in Moorebank, a few hundred metres from our house. You could always go down to Dollar Wal's and get a part for the car for a dollar, sometimes two. It didn't matter if it was a motor or a carburettor, it was one or two dollars, cash.

The owner, Wal, was a horrible sight. He was a big, ugly, grease-covered man in overalls. He didn't wear a shirt underneath and had wads of cash stuffed into his pockets and into his undies. Every now and then Dad would walk us down to Dollar Wal's and buy a ten-dollar bomb for us to drive around the back paddock. This is when we were eight, nine, ten, eleven, twelve years old. The only rule was we had to stay in first gear. A kid from down the road hated that rule, so as soon as we were out of Dad's sight he'd show us how to jam it into second and third and how to spin the wheels. By the time I was twelve I was going sideways around corners.

But this isn't a story where I swing down memory lane and talk about a few kids driving cars in the backyard.

This is about my dad.

It's about masculinity.

It's about idolising a man who wasn't afraid to raise his fists if he thought that his dignity was being threatened. And it's about how that attitude would affect my life.

You see, sometime in the seventies the wrecking industry got taken over by bikies, particularly in the western suburbs. I guess they did it to repurpose stolen cars and to wash the cash they made from the heroin that was just starting to hit the streets.

Riverside Road was soon all wrecking yards and starting to become a real industrial area. Dad despised these new wrecking yard owners because they were out to make a profit, nothing else. They weren't out to help a man or give him the option of buying something cheap secondhand and fixing it up himself. These were important pillars of society to my dad. His version of the Rights of Man.

Maybe Wal died or maybe he sold, but one day he wasn't there. The smell of grease was gone and you had to walk along a line on the polished concrete floor to examine all the old parts that were now cleaned and on the wall. And they sure weren't a buck or two bucks any more. The same carburettor was now twenty dollars. The same water pump cost fifteen.

Dad just hated it. The idea of wrecking yards, according to my dad, was you go into the yard with your tools and you take the part you want off yourself.

So, on a stinking hot day in 1976, we walked into this joint. Straightaway, my dad summed up these three bikies working there. And I knew from his vibe that he wasn't in awe. I was.

There was no doubt about it. These were rough men.

As horrible as Wal might've been, these men were next level. Big, bearded bikie thugs covered in tattoos. For any Millennials it might be hard to imagine, but forty years ago, if you had a tattoo you'd either been in the navy or prison. If you were covered in tattoos, like these men, it was an easily read signal not to mess with 'em. And Dad must've given 'em a look because they had attitude with him which made me really uneasy.

My dad would always start a conversation with, 'How are ya?' and a handshake.

He put out his hand and the first bloke ignored it and said, 'Yeah, mate, whaddya want?'

Well, you might as well have belted my dad over the head with a piece of 4x2 than say that to him. When he offers you his hand and you don't take it you are one second away from copping it like you've never got. My dad was a great boxer. He could handle himself.

We were there to buy a water pump for the mustard yellow '73 Galant I had just bought. Got it cheap 'cause it was covered in hail damage. My first car. Glamorous? Not even close.

And there was the water pump on the wall, all cleaned up.

'Fifteen bucks,' the guy said.

Dad must've been looking for a fight 'cause he said, 'You can stick that up your arse. I'll go down and get one out of the back.'

There was no doubt these blokes were prepping my dad. He looked at me and told me to go to the car and grab his toolbox. As I started to walk away they said, 'Nuh, you can't take your tools down there. You've gotta hire our tools.'

My dad started to fume. You could see it. He was boiling over.

Then they said, 'Go on, use your fucking tools.' They swore at my dad! They swore in front of me! That didn't happen in my world. To Dad, I might as well have been three years old. I could see the veins in his arms and neck pulsing. He was fired up. Dad wasn't a big man, six-two, a middleweight, eighty kilos at best, but weight and size mean nothing when you know how to handle yourself. I've seen fools throw punches that he would slip and slide under. The worst thing you could do was to lift your hands to him. You wouldn't know what came next.

We walked down the back and into the yard. We found this Galant. We took it apart and pulled off the water pump. We cleaned it up and brought it back to the counter. They told my dad it was fourteen bucks.

The one on the wall was fifteen.

They were just egging him on. Three blokes. The biggest one was sitting down with a hideous, smart-arse look on his face. My dad was seeing red but I was with him and he wasn't going to risk a blow-up while I was there.

Still, they push him and they push him. He had no patience anyway. He had two seconds for fools. But he put up with these guys for a long time. Eventually he says, 'I'll give you ten bucks or you can stick it up your arse.'

That's how he said it. He was fired up now. 'Or you can stick it up your arse.'

So he dropped a ten-buck note on the counter and walked off with me and the water pump. Next minute, a tyre wrench skimmed across the ground past us.

They were just trying to shit him even more.

Dad looked at me and said, 'Go to the car.'

I said, 'Don't worry about 'em, Dad.'

He said, 'Go … to … the … car.'

I took the water pump with me and went to the edge of the garage and looked back. He'd lost it. The one who was the mouthiest took a swing at my dad 'cause he knew what was coming. He knew my dad was ready for a blue.

My dad dropped his head under this guy's haymaker, which wouldn't have hurt my dad anyway. Dad could've taken him with one easily, but he jabbed him just so he could straighten him up and give him a proper uppercut. He stood him up straight with the jab and then he lifted him. He literally lifted that guy off the ground. With that, the big guy, who was sitting down drinking Coca-Cola out of a litre bottle, started to stand up and Dad hit him with a straight right and split his nose like a goat's toe, straight across his face. He fell back to his chair unconscious. The other bloke ran. Ran for his life. And Dad said, 'If you throw something at my son again, I'll jam my boot so far up your arse your nose will bleed.'

And I thought, they deserved it, those idiots. That's the thing with boxing. If you know where to place your fists, if they're at the right angle to someone, you can decommission 'em straightaway. Two men were unconscious. Another man was still running out the back somewhere probably looking for more help.

Dad walked back, looked at me and said, 'I told you to get back in the car.'

It's a good story but ten things could've gone wrong. They could've hit my dad with a tyre wrench and killed him. He could've lifted one of those blokes onto the corner of the table and accidently killed him and my dad would be in jail.

I was incredibly proud of my dad. It was a real superhero moment, but it was one of those things that had me raising my fists sooner in life than I should've. I've knocked a few blokes out in my life. I'm not proud of any of those moments.

As a calculated, analytical sorta guy I learned, and yeah it took me a while to learn it, that in life you have to limit your risks and maximise your return.

Here's an example of how I turned a potentially disastrous situation around.

Twenty years later, I was a successful builder. Developments all over Sydney. Every Friday afternoon I'd go to a pub in Paddington, and write all the subcontractors their cheques. I was a healthy, strong man. I didn't take a backward step to anybody. But, still, I was in my mid-thirties and too old to fight, that's for sure.

To put it into perspective, just about every single bloke in that bar, the scaffolders, the plasterers, the brickies, were all working for me and my reputation was strong 'cause I'd cleaned up a few troublemakers here before. And I was standing at the bar when a guy turned around, bumped into me and spilled all his drinks.

And he said, 'You'll be fucking paying for those drinks, mate.'

At that moment, all I could think was, jeez, I was having fun tonight. Why did this idiot have to come along and wreck it? Now I'm going to have to knock his block off. Anybody who talks to you like that is in all sorts of trouble. Warn me you're going to do something and you've limited your options. I don't care if you're six-foot-six. Certain blokes don't do that. These are the blokes that know. They don't threaten you. If you ask for it, they'll finish it quickly. To the loud ones, like this clown, if you offer me a jaw I'll put you to sleep in a second. Now, the thing is, a bar fight is not like in the movies. They get scrappy, anything can happen – hard and fast, and there is no such thing as a good result.

So I said to him, 'No worries, mate. I'll buy those drinks and I'll buy every drink you have tonight and let's get a round of cigars as well.'

He was carrying drinks for five blokes. They were the only blokes in the bar wearing suits and you could tell they thought they were pretty strong. I bought drinks for them and just about everyone in the bar all night.

As the drinks were being pulled, I quietly said, 'Mate, that could've gone nowhere. One of us would've had his head split open and the other one would've been getting hauled off in the back of a cop van. So I'm going to make sure we have the best night we can have.'

My brother Mick, who'd been at the bar, called me up the next day and said, 'Who were those idiots you were with last night? They rang me up from your phone at one in the morning to tell me what a legend you are.'

And I said, 'That's the dickhead who pushed me at the bar.'

That was a good moment in my life. It's a story I tell a lot of young men in their early twenties who remind me of myself, full of testosterone with big chests and ready, too ready, for anything.

Fighting? Who needs it? The best return is to continue the fun time you were having, to offer friendship, a smile, even an apology if you need to.

It's an easy investment for a good return.

5
THE INVENTION THAT (ALMOST) CHANGED THE WORLD

This is a story about my dad's stretcher. It almost changed the world and it just about killed Dad.

By the eighties, Dad's full-time business was design, development and fabrication of medical equipment. Just about every stretcher in every ambulance in this country was built by my dad.

The company was named after Mum and Dad. It was called RLDMA Holdings, which stood for Robert Leo Du Bois Margaret Anne and later became RL & MA Du Bois Engineering.

Dad had bought the company off another bloke. He was winding it up and Dad was working for him. Now, this bloke was the distributor of the stretcher but he was paying other people to make different components of it. In the end,

Dad took over the manufacture of it, and then that bloke worked for Dad as a distributor. It was a bit of a shared business but in the end Dad took it over.

So this is the story. And it's one of the things that broke us.

My mum, my brother, my uncle and a family friend, Bill Polbrook, were all working for the company making stretchers. When the billionaire Kerry Packer had his heart attack and said he'd put defibrillators in all the ambulances, Dad got the contract to make the device to fit the defibrillators into the ambulances. Dad designed the holder and won the contract to build and supply two thousand of them. That's what Dad could do. He could come up with answer for anything. That was a great contract for the business, and for us.

He branched out a little bit. I was going out with a beautician so Dad came up with a waxing table for pregnant women. Sharon had told him, 'What I really need, Bob, is a table to hold a pregnant belly in so they're not uncomfortable, so they can be waxed.'

He came up with that. He sold that.

He made tables for veterinarians. He had a product range going there and it was all off the back of his supply chain for the ambulance stretcher, which was our bread and butter. Dad was starting to do pretty well. He had a couple of delivery trucks. Things were looking up.

The government decided, and a lot of this is written in hindsight, that there was going to be a new stretcher designed and it was going to be sold all over the country. The government developed the specifications and said, if you can come up with a stretcher that meets all these requirements, you'll supply the country for years to come. This was amazing for our business.

Now, we later found out, a company from America had come up with a plan that they had fed to a person of influence to get the contract. And the plan was, 'Create a list of specifications that cannot be fulfilled. You have to ask for something that can't be done. And in the terms of the agreement, give yourself the decision on who gets the contract. If no one can meet the specifications, which they won't be able to, we get it.'

That deal was done.

So they came up with the specifications for a stretcher that enabled you to load a passenger onto the stretcher while it was on the ground. One ambulance officer could work on the patient while the other one lifted it up, manoeuvred it and got it into the ambulance on his own.

Dad just loved that 'cause he had no idea how it could be done. And this had never been done anywhere else on earth. However, it wasn't meant to happen.

My dad could not sleep because this was a problem he needed to solve. He mortgaged the house in Campbelltown, spent all of our savings, and he built a prototype. He built something that met the specifications that they had asked for.

No one, but no one, could fucking believe it.

The hindsight is this. They'd written into the clause, this overriding clause, that regardless ... regardless ... that even if someone came up with a stretcher that met the specifications, a bureaucrat could decide who was going to get the contract because he knew best. Someone with no scientific knowledge.

Let's just put that clause in.

Sure enough, we pumped every cent we had into this. Psychologically, my dad was exhausted. He was completely spent. I reckon he slept one hour at night. He would trial and error, trial and error and trial and error. He'd be at the factory at three o'clock in the morning and he'd come home, have a shower, have some porridge and he would go back.

I'd hear him mutter, 'It didn't work! I was sure this was going to work!' For him it was all in the geometry and mathematics. This was a bloke who couldn't read and write. But he came up with it. And he built a prototype and it worked.

Well, the first thing they said was, 'It's no good because it's got a strap there and we haven't tested if that's a medical-grade strap.'

Well, it was a prototype, obviously.

They just kept coming up with all these problems.

And Dad, being the honest man full of integrity he was, kept thinking, 'Those other stretchers must be amazing because they're putting so much pressure on me!'

The American company hadn't developed anything. They didn't have to. Because they knew they were going to get the contract.

The presentation day came. Dad was so proud. He said, 'Our stretcher was leaps and bounds ahead of the other stretchers. The stretcher company from America, they were just poring all over my stretcher. They were taking photos.'

I was suspicious. I said, 'Why did you let them take photos of it, Dad? It's your stretcher.'

About thirty days after the submission, we got the letter. We'd banked on this. This was a million-dollar contract coming. It was going to get us out of the debt we were in.

Sure enough, they'd chosen the American stretcher. Ferno-Washington was going to supply stretchers to Australia for eternity.

Signed off. Done deal.

My dad had a nervous breakdown. We'd lost everything. We had to shut the door of the factory. We were going to lose our home.

I went to the radio jock Alan Jones and asked him to help. The government was pumping this 'Buy Australia' shit, pumping it like you wouldn't believe. My friend's father was the head of the 'Buy Australia' campaign. He told me there was nothing he could do. Alan Jones wasn't interested in talking about it. I went to John Laws. I went to the *Today Tonight* show. No one was interested in this story!

My dad was broken and he lost the plot. All he did was sulk. The Black Dog had hit him. He was depressed and lost. He was a failed man. Something that he thought was amazing, and was fucking amazing, was rejected and he was confused.

He was confused with the world and he was confused with the country that he loved so much. Confused with the system that he believed in. That these people would do this to a man. What happened was, yeah, we had met the specifications in every single point, the American company hadn't, but a bureaucrat made the decision that a better choice would be the American stretcher.

And there it was.

I remembered the knock at the door some time later because I was home visiting my parents. I went to see who it was and this guy said, 'My name is so and so and I represent Ferno-Washington.'

Dad yelled from across the house, 'Oh, you can piss off.'

Dad hated that name Ferno-Washington, he hated America now because they'd got the contract over him for a stretcher he believed was a piece of shit. And it was, because it never fucking got used here. It was that bad.

And this guy said, 'I understand you are upset but we recognise that you've created something that is twenty years ahead of its time and we want to buy it.'

Dad said, 'Mate, sod off. Get your book and yourself and piss off.'

Dad was riled up. I went out there and said to the bloke, 'What's going on? Why don't you just leave him alone?'

He said, 'I just want to explain. We understand what's happened here. And what we'd like to do is this. I've been instructed by my boss, Mr Dick Ferneau, in Cincinnati – he's heard about your dad. He's seen what he has created, we've seen some photographs. He wants to fly your dad and mum out to America. We'll pay for everything, we'll pay your costs, whatever it takes. This bloke wants to meet your dad. He's created something that is twenty years ahead of its time.'

Now, that was a relief for me. But my dad was even more confused. He said, 'Piss off. Get out of my house. You screwed me over and you screwed over my family.'

And the guy said, 'We've done none of that. Can I come in and talk to you?'

He'd summed Dad up pretty well. I told him my dad had health issues. He'd been seeing a psychiatrist. He was punching walls and wanted to kill people. We'd got into a debt we couldn't pay. We were broke.

The guy came in and said, 'We want to help you out. We realise you've been screwed over.'

Dad exploded. 'Bullshit! They wouldn't screw us over!'

The guy replied, 'You play it as you see it. We knew we were going to get this contract before the tender went out. We helped set the specifications so no one could meet them. And we acknowledge that you have met them. Let's just forget what happened here because it ain't going to change.'

My dad believed in democracy. He believed in the system. He believed in unionism. He believed in Labor and Liberal and arguing and the balance of power. He believed in that and this guy just came in and pissed on it all.

There were no ethics in our country. Nothing. Zero. Dad just despised it.

I said, 'Dad, this is an opportunity that these guys are offering. We're in a bit of strife financially.'

The guy said, 'We've been instructed to buy the patents off you for whatever you want. Bob, you can name your price here.' And he was being really honest.

My dad was a two-bit sorta guy with a factory in West Hoxton Park and a multi-billionaire had recognised that my dad was a genius and wanted to help him out. That may seem realistic today but back then it didn't. It was beyond any realm of rational thought. We didn't even know what a billionaire was, really, unless it was Kerry Packer.

Alan Jones wasn't interested in us. John Laws wasn't interested in us. But this American billionaire was. None of it made sense.

My dad said, 'I don't have any patents.'

The guy said, 'Okay, what we'll do is that we'll get the patents for you, in your name and then we'll buy them off you.'

Dad said, 'Why would you do that? What are you up to?'

Dad was so cynical.

The man said, 'We recognise what you've done and we believe it should be recognised.'

They flew me and Mum and Dad first class on Qantas to Cincinnati and shipped Dad's prototype stretcher to America as well. Mr Ferneau, who was about eighty years old, met us at the office. He was still on the board and was one of the richest men in America.

He was just like my dad. Here was this guy who had started off repairing pushbikes and motorbikes in his garage with his mate El Bourgraf. There's a photo of them in their t-shirts and they look like Dad. They look like the same guys.

Mr Ferneau said, 'Bob, can you just demonstrate your stretcher for the R & D team?'

We didn't know what R & D team meant. Mr Ferneau explained it meant research and development and that there were forty people in the team. And he looked at Dad and said in these long American vowels, 'Do you maaaaaand, Baaaaaab, if the team asks you some questions?'

Dad said they could ask anything.

Mr Ferneau asked if Dad could demonstrate how the stretcher worked with an ambulance. Dad being Dad, rolled up his sleeves, moved a few tables around, did this, did that, and explained that in Australia that's the height of where most people's hands fall and therefore the height of the ambulance door.

One of the R & D team asked Dad if it was the mandated height of all ambulance stretchers.. He said he didn't know but he assured 'em it was right.

There were a few guffaws and you could feel the scepticism in the crowd.

Mr Ferneau said, 'How do you know that, Bob?'

We were in trouble already.

Dad picked a tall bloke and a short bloke and asked 'em to stand up for a sec and to put their hands beside them. And there you go, most people's hands hang at the same height.

Mr Ferneau stared and said, 'Well, I'll be goddaaaaaaaaamned!'

Dad wheeled the stretcher in and the rest of it went like clockwork. Everybody cheered at the end. It was one of the proudest days of my life.

Mr Ferneau said, 'Bob, I've seen enough. Let's go to the club.' Then he looked over at his secretary and told her to take Mum shopping. They came back later with trench coats (it was a brutal mid-winter in the American mid-west) and all sorts of things we never wore again. Later, Mum was taken to the beauty parlour while Dad and Mr Ferneau got pissed.

I stayed behind and talked to the business manager. I had a fair understanding of business at that stage and had put a proposal together. He pulled me aside and said, 'Listen, Barry, Mr Ferneau has already given us the go ahead for an offer much larger than that.'

I'd worked the proposal out on how much we needed to get Mum and Dad out of debt. I said something like two hundred and fifty grand and they said, 'No, no, we'll give you two hundred and fifty grand right now.' They got our account details and literally transferred it straightaway but what they wanted was to identify all the things that could be patented.

'Once we get those, Mr Ferneau wants to buy the patents off your dad.'

So that was another two hundred and fifty grand.

Then the guy said, 'And what Mr Ferneau wants to do is pay Bob five thousand a month for the rest of his life.'

Dad wouldn't take it.

He said, 'I'll come and work for ya, but I don't want you to just give me money.'

I said, 'We … will … take it.'

And what they did was, they gave Dad a video camera and told him, whenever you have an idea, just make it, video it, and send the information back and we will share the profits

That made Dad happy, because Dad didn't want something for nothing.

So what happened to the amazing stretcher?

They sold four hundred to Saudi Arabia, which was a big cheque.

But the cost of re-training ambulance officers to use the stretchers, particularly in the American system which was privatised, was too prohibitive to allow its introduction. They used the patented parts in many products. It ended up being used by computer salesmen who could wheel computers into offices on it, and by funeral parlours, in many areas.

The stretcher was never mass-produced. Because it was too advanced.

And the government? Again, that's why I'm cynical about shit. It's the reason I question everything. If someone says, take an antibiotic, I say, why? Because self-interest always gets the inside run, whether it's a developer, Big Pharma or a manufacturer. It's as simple as that.

You can't rely on the ethics and integrity of men like my dad any more.

Because they don't exist.

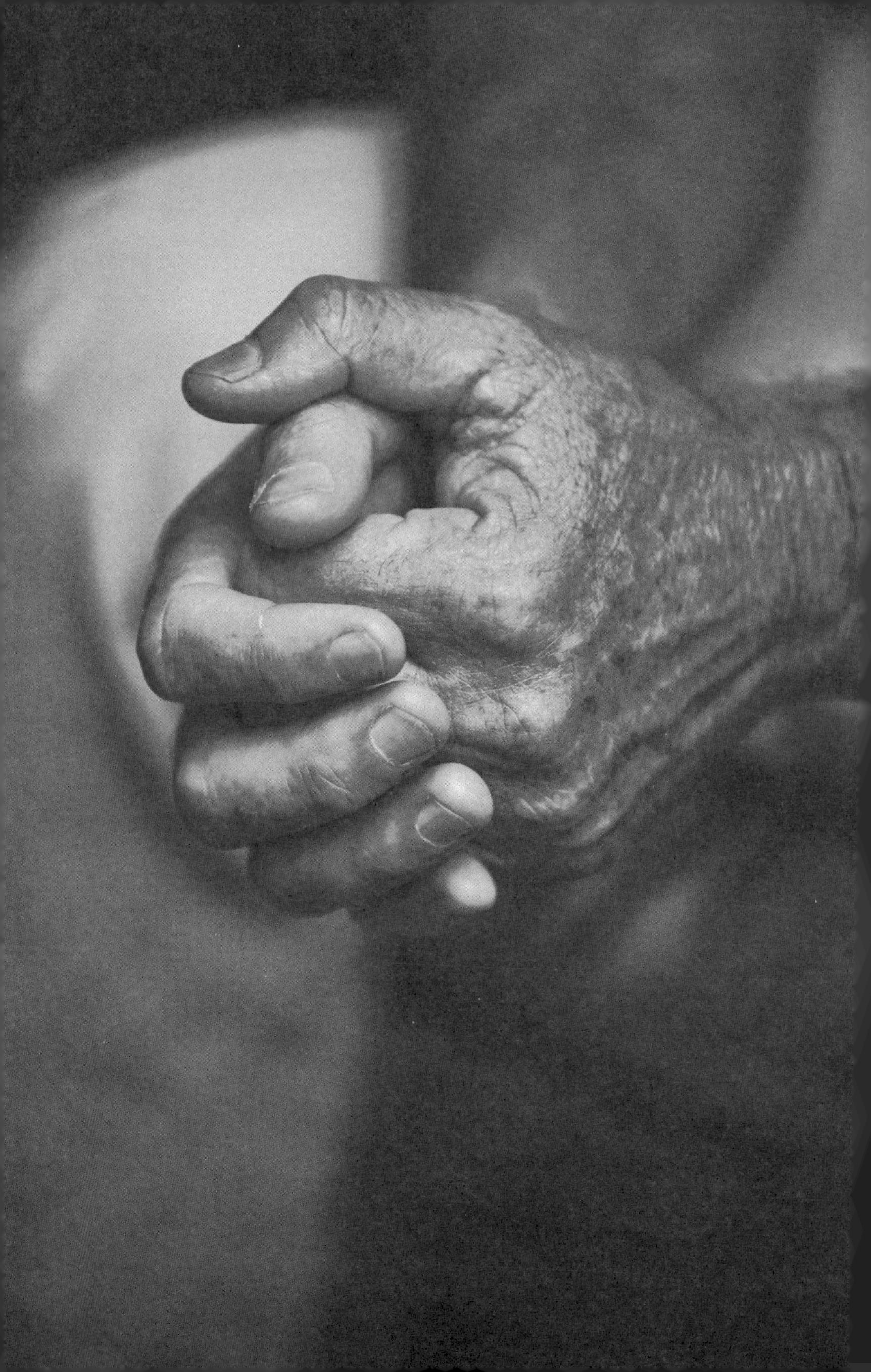

6
LEARNING TO FLY

It's not the fall that gets you, they say, but the sudden stop at the end. In the wet Sydney summer of 2000, I slipped and fell fourteen metres off a beachfront apartment building – the height where it's fifty-fifty if you live or die – onto concrete.

The memory of the fall is vivid: gasping for air and trying to feel my feet, praying I wasn't going to be in a chair, rain smashing me in the face and a girl staring out of the next door apartment building, screaming.

But let's backtrack a little. How did I get there?

The building I launched myself off was the last block of apartments on the headland of Ben Buckler at the very eastern point of North Bondi. It's not an exaggeration to call it the greatest piece of real estate in Australia. Twenty minutes to the guts of our biggest city. Iconic beach right there. No one's going to block your view here. The next hunk of land is New Zealand.

The building was the smallest in the street, two storeys at the street level and three as it terraced down to the boat ramp. For sale was a small two-bedder.

Because of the building's size, and being a developer, I knew I could get council approval to build a penthouse on top. Getting strata to okay these sorts of things can be a hellish battle, of course. You need to get seventy-five percent of the unit owners to agree on what is called a special resolution.

Fifty percent ain't hard. Three-quarters can be an impossibility as greed and envy and every other dark human emotion comes out to play. You can offer the world and, still, strata owners will have that look that screams suspicion, that somehow they're getting screwed, that someone is in cahoots with someone else.

When I had a look at the body corp's notes I found out that two women owned the rest of the building. They didn't talk to each other, had been fighting for twenty years in fact, and the building was in atrocious shape.

Leaks. Concrete cancer. A roof like a sieve. It needed at least a hundred grand's worth of remedial work.

And me, being the negotiator that I am, and a person that believes you can communicate with anybody, saw ... opportunity.

So I bought into the bottom floor as a rental apartment, as another piece for my portfolio and went along to the first body corporate meeting. It was like I imagined: the two women didn't want to look at each other and both had inherited their apartments, which was interesting. One woman lived there, the other one didn't get much rent for her three apartments because the building was so poorly maintained. It had no money in the sinking fund.

It was one of those times when the market had just gone off the boil and property was cheap so, typically, I bought the two-bedder. If I got the approval, great, if I didn't, I wasn't going to lose my shirt.

At the body corporate meeting I told 'em there was a ton of issues with this building and we'd have to find the money from somewhere to fix it. Both of 'em said, fine, but we're not going to pay a thing. I felt all this aggression. They didn't speak to each other, only through other people. It was the classic, she won't pay so I won't pay scenario. Both were asset rich and cash poor.

I said, 'You know, girls, I have an idea here. I'm a builder and I know it's going to cost a hundred grand to replace the roof. I've got an idea for you. I'll fix the roof for free and renovate the entire building but in return I would like to have the space within the roof and take the opportunity to create a unit there.'

They saw they could get the place fixed up for free, which would increase the value of their apartments considerably. I saw that I was going to make a lot of money.

Both of 'em didn't believe that it was possible to get a penthouse through council so we made an agreement. Even if I failed with the development approval I'd agree to fix the roof. It was a hundred-thousand-dollar gamble.

We agreed.

And as it happened, the girls wanted to offload a few more of their units so a friend and I bought 'em.

I put the development application into council and got permission for a 245-square-metre penthouse plus balconies. Without lifting a hammer, I'd made a lot of money. I was doing well financially but you can always use a little more money. That was my mind space.

We started building and it was a summer sodden by those tropical rains that slip further south every decade or so. A savage storm came through when Leonie, whom I'd just married, and I were still living in the building.

It's the night of my fall. A few of the units are vacant and have been leaking like hell. I've been out a dozen times trying to identify where the leak was coming from. With the heavy rain pounding the roof, this is finally a chance to follow where the water is coming from.

When you have a leak, often where the drip is isn't where the root of the problem is. Leonie tells me I am crazy to be climbing onto the roof in the storm.

I tell her, 'I'll be right, love, it'll be fine.'

It's a three-storey building on the street at this stage and five-storeys on the beachside. Leonie pushes.

'Baby, I'm really worried, I'm really worried.'

In my typical jokey way, I say, 'Listen, if you hear a bang, call an ambulance.'

I strap a little bit of rope to my waist and up I go.

Soon I am standing on the highest peak of the plywood roof, at the top of the curve. It has a tarp over it but it's very slippery. The horizon is a grey sea of big waves. I look at the sky. There's lightning and thunder and pouring rain. I'm already soaking wet when a shard of light pushes through the clouds and I see a green film over the ply. Just as I notice it, my body goes tense and as it stiffens I move a fraction and I think, 'Oh shit, if I slip here, if I start to slide, there's nothing for me to grab hold of.'

I have the realisation that, 'This isn't good, this isn't good … at all.'

And the more I think about it, the more I tense up. This is all happening within a couple of seconds, of course: look at the sky, see the mould, think oh shit. The next thing I know my legs are above my head and I'm sliding flat-out towards the edge of the fourteen-metre drop.

We have scaffolding all around the outside of the building and there are these 150 mil by 40 mil planks that are supposed to stop things … in this case me … from falling off the edge.

It's interesting how sharp your thoughts get, how focused, and how time really does slow down, when you're about to die. As I crash through the planks, which don't slow me by the way, I reach for a bar. My middle finger and ring finger snap straight backwards.

I keep falling.

I think to myself, 'Well, big fellow, this is going to be tough.'

I look over my shoulder and I'm in the air. I've completely cleared the scaffolding and I hit the unit block next door, catching my feet and putting my head closer to the ground.

Another thought: 'Mate, even you can't pull this one off. You're fucked.'

And then: 'Why now? I'm just about there. I've got all this stuff happening. I've just gotten married. It can't be the time.'

I also feel a terrible guilt that Leonie is going to see me with my head smashed open. With that thought, I wrap my hands around my head.

BARRY DU BOIS & MIGUEL MAESTRE

I hit the concrete.

My hands come off my head and it slaps hard onto the ground. Then my body hits so hard my ankle opens up. I snap the ankle bone, my ribs, a shoulder. Two fingers are wrenched out of their sockets and three vertebrae break.

I lie there. There isn't even half an ounce of air in my lungs. I gasp for air. I don't know if the girl next door is screaming because I'm covered in blood or because she doesn't know what has just happened.

Seconds later, I'm surrounded by people. No one wants to move me.

Is he dead? Is he paralysed?

The ambulance arrives after maybe fifteen minutes. I tell the driver to cover me, that I'll be alright, and for him to get out of the rain.

He laughs and says he isn't leaving me.

I don't tell anyone how worried I am that I'm paralysed. It's been twenty minutes since the fall. It's cold, I'm wet, and I can't feel any sensation in my legs.

I ask the ambo if he can see me moving my feet, and if I'm paralysed.

He tells me I'm okay.

I feel an overwhelming relief.

They chuck me in the ambulance and we bolt to St Vincent's hospital, fifteen minutes away when you've got a siren and flashing lights. It's a busy Thursday night in Emergency and I lay there for two hours, soaking wet, until a doc comes to see me, puts a cast on my leg and leaves.

I'm 186 centimetres and I have bruises from my heels to my head. All my back. The bottom of my arms. My calves. My hamstrings. The bottom of my feet are black. I piss blood. It's clear I have extensive injuries but, being me, I have no interest in spending the night at the hospital. I'm forty years old and I've never been in a hospital. I don't wanna start now.

I ask someone, an orderly maybe, what happens next.

They tell me to lie there and … wait.

I've been lying on this bed for six hours and I'm still soaking wet. I'm freezing cold. I look at Leonie and ask her to get me out of here. The last thing she wants to do is to take me out of hospital without any sort of rigorous examination. Under duress, I can be a pushy sonofabitch sometimes, so she gets me in a wheelchair, down to the exit and checks me out.

I'm told I have to go back and see a specialist in a week or so.

I go home and lie in bed.

Two weeks later, the specialist discovers the three compressed fractures in my back. Surprisingly, he doesn't tell me only to rest, although this is important during the six-week healing process, but also to move, to get strong. I'm in the middle of a couple of big developments so this is good news. It's not a time when I can take a lot of time off.

Soon, I'm strapping myself into the office chair and wheeling myself around the penthouse, working, moving. Pain is a funny thing. I'm scared to walk because it hurts so much.

I have great friends and a loyal staff but, mentally and physically, that pain gets to you and it's easy to take short cuts.

I start to pack on the weight.

Six-nine months later, I'm driving to my developments, and it hurts like hell to get in and out of the car, so I fill the tank with fuel and grab whatever I am going to eat from the service station. The food from servos isn't exactly organic or even vaguely nourishing. Mars bars. Packaged white-bread sandwiches. Bottles of Coke. Dirty, empty calories. It keeps me alive and moving but at the cost of a tyre wrapped around my waist. The classic old guy gut. And when you're eating too much sugar you're reducing the ability of your immune system to fight sickness. It clouds your ability to think clearly or with any sort of intellectual rigour.

I struggle. The pain doesn't let up. I have therapy to get rid of the bruising. The scar tissue that comes with a fall like that is phenomenal. I'm still pissing blood. I don't want to sound like a wanker but I ignore that shit.

Hurt isn't always physical.

It was only two years before that my nieces were let down by friends and by society. Soon, my mum, my beautiful mother, will be diagnosed with cancer. My treasured wife's cancer will mean she's unable to have children.

My head is everywhere.

The clouds move in. Nieces. My broken body. I'm fat. Chasing money and for what?

I refuse to stop. Maybe it's to my detriment, maybe it's a strength. I figure if you punch through things you'll come good at the end.

It's a combination of naivety and self-deception.

It doesn't always work.

7
DEPRESSION

Here's the thing. Depression doesn't announce its arrival. It's not like it's there one minute and gone the next.

My fall into what felt like a darkness where nothing good existed was a result of a combination of things: my nieces had been interferred with and what followed was a brutal insight into how the legal system works or, in our case, didn't work. I'd fallen off the building and was in agony and couldn't control my weight gain. Mum had been in and out of illness for a decade, first breast cancer, then stomach cancer, and then she died in front of my eyes.

Leonie and I had been trying desperately for children but suffered miscarriage after miscarriage, all late miscarriages, often twins. It went from heartbeats and smiles in the obstetrician's rooms to late-night screams in the toilet. And then there was her cervical cancer. As much as it was the wrong time to give up, I gave up. Leonie had to deal with it all on her own.

I remember talking to a psychiatrist about this in 2006. I gave him the whole catalogue of woe and he pointed out that any one of those things – the abuse of my nieces, Mum dying, my fall, the inability to have kids, Leonie having cancer – could have driven me to depression.

'But you've got 'em all.'

The realisation of what happened to the girls, and the struggle that followed, unbalanced me. I wanted to fix the world. But it's an unfixable world. I was surfing one day down at Werri Beach on the NSW South Coast and there was this older bloke pushing a couple of kids onto waves.

I said, 'Mate, fucking … move … away from those kids.'

He said, 'They're my nephews!'

I was aggressive with him 'cause I didn't trust anybody. I still don't. I wouldn't trust anyone with my children. I suspected everybody. That's the first part of depression. When you start to think the world is against you.

We couldn't have children. My wife and I, of all people. A healthy beautiful personal trainer who has an amazing diet, who is dying to be a mother, and me, virile, healthy, never smoked, didn't drink too much. All of a sudden we had to go to IVF to have children.

When you go to IVF you don't make love any more. It's this structure and process of dates and times and temperatures and drugs and it's the last thing that my wife and I imagined when we thought of having children. We always imagined a child being born through love and romance and affection and touch and warmth and understanding and caring.

That's a child.

We were in this process where I'd jab a needle in her sixty times a month. Every day, two needles. They'd do the blood tests, call us up and say, 'Okay, you're about to ovulate … now go and have sex.'

I couldn't stomach it after a while.

When you're a kid and you go in a running race, you give it your best and you're happy with that. All of a sudden, you're giving your best to the most important thing in the world to you and it's not happening.

Then came the loss of my mum. I'd lost my mum and I couldn't have children. What was I here for? What was my role on this earth other than to be a slave to society?

That imbalance was overwhelming.

My mum thought she'd live forever and she'd see my children grow up. For a guy who had everything, all he wanted was his mum to hold his child.

I had no faith in regional hospitals so I brought Mum to a doctor in Sydney. The highly respected doctor looked at her file and said, 'Maybe if I'd seen her two years ago this wouldn't be the same story. But your mum's got twenty-eight to thirty days to go. If she lives that long.'

He suggested we take her home or somewhere comfortable where she could spend her last few weeks. That wasn't what was supposed to happen.

Most of us have this feeling of how things will turn out in the world. One day, long into the future, we'll get a phone call to say our dad has passed, that he was happy until the end. Several years later, after travelling the world, we'll be surrounding our mum in bed, everyone smiling. We'll kiss her on the forehead and she'll gently go to sleep.

I don't know how many other people have that vision but I did. And there she was, my beautiful mum who never hurt anybody in her life, in immense pain, and a doctor whom I'd rightly put a lot of faith into saying, 'No, Baz. I'm sorry. There's nothing I can do for your mum. It's over.'

This guy was going to be our saviour. I had told the family he was the best and that's what Mum deserved. I stared at him and said, loudly, aggressively, 'NO! No ... That can't be right. It's not her time. You must be able to do something. Please, I don't want to hear that.' I wanted to belt him.

The doctor apologised, told me he was busy and left.

I was so fucking mad at the world at this stage. I told my brother and my sister what the doctor had said and then we took Mum to a hospice in Goulburn. I spent as much time with her as I possibly could. I watched her gasp for air as she drowned in her own secretions.

And that was how she died.

One week into it, I was hoping her next breath of life was her last. It took three weeks of that before she gasped one more time and died amid the screams from the dementia patients in the same ward. Horrible.

To go from that to putting needles into your wife for IVF tore me up. I wasn't sure I wanted to be here. I loved my wife, my dad was still around, I loved my brother and sister and my friends, but I felt like I was to blame because this didn't seem to happen to anybody else. Maybe I was the cog that was fucking everything up.

I was dark.

I told Leonie I wasn't sure that I loved her any more. I told her I didn't want to go on together, that we weren't going to have children and it was impossible for us to be happy. I left her a couple of times. I walked out and said, 'I don't know what I'm doing but I'm not coming back.'

It was ridiculous. I still had a beautiful home, I had wonderful friends, a loving wife, work was great.

I remember this clearly. I was sitting in front of my car overlooking the beach next to my house at North Bondi. I'd had enough. I was contemplating driving down the coast to kill the bloke who'd interfered with the girls.

The darkness.

If I couldn't do that, I considered just driving and not stopping. I thought, with me gone everyone would be better off. How I could consider Leonie would be better off without me there, I don't know. I felt that with our savings and if she just sold a few things she could have a lovely life without me.

I don't think I ever really considered taking my own life but I didn't want to be Baz any more. I just wanted to leave my world and became a wanderer, to go places where people didn't know me.

As I was sitting there my phone rang. It was my mate Gaz. He'd worked as an apprentice for me years before. He was a bull of a man. Had four daughters. He was a fair bit younger than me but he was someone I'd always respected and

BARRY DU BOIS & MIGUEL MAESTRE

looked up to. He reminded me of a cross between me and my dad.

I said, 'What are ya up to, Gaz?'

He said, 'Well, it's Thursday so we're out of money.'

Like most young couples, they were in debt to their eyeballs and lived on nothing. Doing the best they could.

Gaz said, 'We're out of money but Simone's making toasted sandwiches and I'm heading down to the bottle-o to buy four beers.'

All of a sudden, I had a thought. This was the simple life that I remembered when I was living in that little house on the six-lane highway. We'd have toasted sandwiches and a cup of tea. The special sandwiches were the banana ones with sugar on them.

And I felt a wave of warmth break over me. I burst into tears and said to myself, 'That's what I want. This life is never going to give it to me.'

I told Leonie I couldn't stand it any more.

Leonie asked me see a doctor friend mine of mine. I knew it would be a waste of time. And, sure enough, he straightaway suggested I go on anti-depressant drugs. We both walked out of there and I said, 'Babe, if anti-depressants are where this guy thinks I've got to go, I've gotta change everything 'cause I'm so far off track it's not funny.'

Leonie had always insisted a poor diet and a lack of exercise had a lot to do with my depression. She begged my best friend Rod and my brother Mick to talk to me. They went on this campaign to make me admit that I was depressed.

I refused to do it. You don't think you're depressed. You think everybody is against you and they're wrong.

I hated the government. God help you if you were a parking cop near me. I'd happily take on any confrontation. I was so aggressive that if someone said something to me that I didn't like they'd quickly realise it wasn't a place they wanted to go.

Through all this, I was working the hardest I've ever worked. Four hours' sleep a night. Leonie could see me spiralling. She told me I wasn't the guy she knew. The rock she loved. And she asked, 'How do we get that other person back that used be so happy?'

She bugged me about food. About eating sugar. Not having too many coffees. When you're working twenty hours a day, you're living on coffee and sugar.

Yet the success of the business had created a veneer of happiness. When we work with R U OK, a lot of the losses we have through suicide are people who on the surface are doing really, really well. My friends and my colleagues thought I was killing it: sports cars, lots of people working for me, money to burn.

And on the surface I was killing it. But nothing was working.

Then, after more discussion with Leonie, Mick and Rod, who are normally the sorts of guys who would say, 'She'll be right,' changed their attitude. They said to me, 'We need to know you're okay.'

I said, 'Why? What's wrong? Don't tell me there's something wrong with me.'

And they told me what a big part I was of so many people's lives, of the people I help, all the people who love me, the workers whose lives pivoted around my business.

And I admitted it.

I said, 'I am struggling.'

It was funny. Mick and I worked together but you can have life and you can have work in two different places. He saw me ten hours a day and didn't know I was depressed.

And, then, I saw the massive crash coming in the economy in 2007. We call it the GFC now but it was just 'Armageddon' back then. I told Leonie, listen, there's a crash coming and whether I'm here or not, there's an opportunity to shore up our future here. The stock market was at record highs. Real estate was at record highs. I knew it would crash and I knew it would crash hard. I didn't want any tangible assets. I wanted cash.

I sold just about everything we owned. I'd been sailing a lot with my close friend and mentor Fraser that year and I had started to find happiness at sea.

Then I had a colonic irrigation. I didn't know the person who was doing it, but she was a younger lady and she was heavily pregnant. The people who work in wellness centres are usually pretty broadminded. I blurted my guts out to her, about Leonie's miscarriages, my mum dying of cancer, the girls. I was talking to a complete stranger and I remember … unloading …

… If you'll excuse the pun …

… so much stuff and I got a calmness out of that. And after listening to me, she told me that Leonie was right, that food plays a big part of your overall wellness. I'd been eating so much crap over the previous ten years it didn't surprise me when she massaged my stomach and, through a clear tube, all this horrible black stuff started coming out of my body.

After that, I gave in to Leonie's diet. I got into my surfing. My back started to free up from all the sailing. I was starting to come good.

This was one of the straws that started to rebuild the camel's back. The good food, the love and support I had from my wife. When you treat someone terribly and they keep fighting for you, it's an incredible feeling. She never gave up on me.

What Leonie did for me was greater than any gift or holiday or grand proclamation of love.

All these tiny things seemed to get a snowball effect going. All of a sudden I wasn't hurting as much. I was looking better again.

I was eating well and I was moving my body so I was sleeping better. I started Bikram yoga and maybe it's a placebo effect but every time I stepped out of that overheated room I felt like I'd washed out some of the bad.

Good things were happening to me.

Financially, we were in a good place.

I took Dad and my brother to Paris to see the yacht I'd bought.

I started to open up.

I'd drifted into depression and I'd come out. Delusion had pushed me in but reality had brought me back.

My lowest moment is hurting someone else. You can't hurt me. Which may not make sense 'cause I'm writing about how badly I was hurting but I was hurt because I was failing others.

I failed to save my mum. My mum was the third youngest in her family and the rest are still alive. Her dad only died a few years ago and he was 102 years old. How is that fair that my mum, the sweetest person on earth, passed away in 2004 yet people who have done nothing for this planet are still here?

I failed to save my nieces. I failed to save my wife.

When you're the alpha male and things go wrong around you, there's only one person to blame. You.

That's not right, but that's what I did.

As soon as I got into TV I got involved with R U OK because the philosophy of creating meaningful conversations, of engaging with the person and making 'em aware that you heard them, and then following up and offering assistance if they need it, saved me.

My loved ones did it and it worked. I'm here.

LIFE FORCE

8
DRIFTING WITH FRASER

When I was seven, Dad bought an old plywood boat at an auction. The transom was rotted out but it had half a cabin so we could all sleep on it. This was theoretical, of course, because it wasn't even seaworthy yet. We parked it in the garage and Mum, Dad and us three kids would go in and sand the boat while we saved up to buy the paint to finish it off with.

It was a two-year project. Every day after school, on weekends, during holidays and at night, we were down there with our sanding blocks and, later, with paint brushes.

I had just turned nine when we finished it and we took it down to Burrinjuck Dam there on the Murrumbidgee River out the back of Canberra. It was great. Just great. I remember it so clearly I tear up if I think about it.

But that was how we did things. We loved boats but we couldn't afford one so we all worked hard and we made it happen. Every year we'd save up and catch the train to the Hordern Pavilion Boat Show in the city. Dad would always complain that the admission price had gone up again and the bastards were ripping us off.

Still.

We were always one of the first families there. Dreams are free, right? Not that we would ever over-dream. Every boat that was remotely in our capability of saving for, we would take our shoes off and patiently wait our turn to climb on board and sit in those cabins and dream that one day we'd sail away.

When you're a kid, that sense of belonging and security gives you the opportunity to dream. You don't have to give kids Playstations and toys. All you have to do is give them the opportunity to dream and to flourish in their own imaginations.

And the lesson I learned from all that was, I had to have a boat.

Fast-forward to 2004. I was forty-four years old, fat and depressed as fuck.

I kept having that memory of the Hordern Pavilion Boat Show. That was one of the memories that gave me relief from some of the pain I was in.

A friend of mine from North Bondi, Udo, is a boat salesman. I called him up and said, 'Mate, I just want to get something I can do up with Dad.' I thought if I could find a tender, a little boat, Dad and I might be able to have a weekend here and there polishing the deck, screwing in new stainless steel fittings and painting the deck in the summer sun. All those romantic thoughts we have about boats.

I wanted my nephew Callum to be near Dad and to get some of the wisdom and discipline that I didn't think I had. Dad, Mick and I put a little outboard on the boat and we motored it from Rose Bay in Sydney Harbour to a waterfront property I'd bought at Middle Harbour in Seaforth. That was where it was going to stay and that was where we were going to restore it. What I didn't consider was Dad living on the South Coast and the overwhelming nature of my work. It was an impossible dream. We never touched it again.

But through the process of buying the little boat, Udo had asked me if I'd like to try Twilight Sailing on Wednesday nights. He said if I was planning on buying a bigger boat, something significant, I should try the group sailing thing out so I could pick up a few things. The way it works is when a boat dealer sells a boat to someone, he helps 'em find like-minded souls to help race the boat. It's a win-win for both parties. As any boat owner will tell you, finding people to crew it, particularly something big, ain't easy. And for the crew member, you learn how to sail and you get to check out the boats.

Now. The boat I got onto wasn't a bad little boat. It was small and the bunch of blokes I was with weren't my sort of driven, win-at-all costs kinda men, although the owner was a nice bloke. Not that I was much better. My back was still raw from the fall. I was hurting. And I weighed 120 kilos. All that weight put incredible pressure on my compressed fractures.

But I'd always pictured myself on a winning boat, something that befitted the status I had of myself in my head. Even though I hadn't done a lot of sailing I believed I'd be good at it.

I straightaway let these guys know I believed I was good at sailing and that I should probably steer and do the important jobs. They weren't alpha males so I quickly rose to the top of the little pile.

On our first twilight sail, I looked around and thought, 'It's not much of a boat but it's the boat I'm in. I'm going to make the most of it.' I had to stretch and move a lot on that first night and I knew I was going to be in pain the next day but it didn't matter. I had to do something. The following morning, I felt a bit of a muscle twinge in my stomach and in my biceps. I was sore, but it was a good sore.

I felt good about myself for the first time in a long time. Over the next two weeks I began to feel elevated. Then, on the third week, Udo invites this new bloke onto the boat, an older man called Fraser Johnston.

When he comes onto the boat, Udo nudges me and says, 'We're going to win tonight.' We'd never finished better than second last.

I say, 'How do you figure that? Do we get a motor?'

He goes, 'Better than a motor. Fraser's on.'

'Who the fuck is Fraser?'

I see this bloke and I watch him. I sum people up really quickly. The owner of the boat proudly hands the wheel over to Fraser. I watch him closely, thinking, 'What's this old fart doing?'

He looks over his shoulder at me and says, 'Bloke, pass that bucket to me.'

Bloke!

I think, 'Okay, I'm Baz, I'm sort of running this show. I'm the top dog here.' And all of a sudden, I'm just 'bloke'. I've been shot down the hierarchy. I need him to know that I am more important than all the other blokes on the boat but he isn't interested.

He says, 'You're the bloke who lost his mum?'

I say, 'Yeah, I am.'

'We're going to get along well,' he replies. 'I like you already. Now pass me that bucket, Bloke.'

As it turns out, Fraser had arrived before anyone else. He'd surveyed the boat and went through it from the bilge up.

I learned more about preparation that night than I've ever learned in my life. He was down there squeezing the greasy water out of the bilge, cleaning it, loving the boat he was about to take control of. He needed to check every seacock, every ribbing in the hull, the lines, the sails. It was the minutiae of his preparation that impressed me. He'd pick up a line and tell the owner, 'This one's no good. It'll be okay this week, but it needs to be replaced.' He went through a complete check of the boat, something I never would have done.

It was an amazing night. We were a cog in a machine that was unstoppable. He swore at us with so much venom through the race it was unbelievable. He called us every fucking piece of shit there is. My only job … only job … that night was make sure that the headsail got from port to starboard without fouling when we tacked. In Fraser's opinion, I didn't do it right once.

I'd never been talked to like that in my whole life. But we won the race by a country mile. When we made the last turn to go downwind, we were so far in front it wasn't funny. On a boat that always came closer to last than first. It blew my mind that we could achieve so much in one night.

Afterwards, he sat with each man on the boat and went through the race, tack for tack, and calmly explained everything they did right and how they could do better, and the things they didn't do as well and why they didn't do them as well.

It was the best grilling of my life. And I thought, 'I really want to be around this guy.' He sat with me at the front of the boat and he said, 'I heard you've had a tough time. If you want to talk, I would like you to know that you can always call me.'

This is a guy I summed up as a bit of a dick and out to win an opportunity. He was a self-made man, wealthy. You wouldn't know it to look at him, but he didn't give a shit about what someone thought about him. He cared about the sea, he cared about the environment and he cared about humanity.

One afternoon he said to me, 'Why don't you come drifting with me, Baz?'

I didn't know what drifting was.

'Well, when I'm not doing this, I deliver yachts around the world,' he said. 'It's a great place to think.'

'I'd love to do that,' I told him.

'Next week I'm taking a boat from Sydney to Hamilton Island and you're welcome to join me.'

I went home, and I said to Leonie, 'I don't know if you'll like this or not, but next week I'm going to sail a boat from Sydney to Hamilton Island.'

'Who you going there with?'

I said, 'It's this bloke I met at sailing. I see him as an amazing mentor and he reminds me of Dad. He swears at me but I really am drawn to him.'

Classic Leonie, my beautiful wife, said, 'Babe, whatever you've got to do, do it. If you think it'll help you, do it.'

One week later, I arrived at the port with thousands of dollars of equipment I'd bought just for the trip. Stuff no one could possibly need. I had handheld compasses. I had two different outfits for each day. I had wind shears. I had special gloves for sailing at night and special gloves for sailing in the day. I had a solar charger for my computer. I had more equipment than you would take on a world cruise and all secured in two really nice big bags.

I arrived wearing the classic white polo-neck jumper after going through every sailing magazine that I could find to determine how a sailor should look.

Fraser's whole life is in a duffel bag. It has a net, a knife, a compass, a few t-shirts and shorts.

For various reasons, Fraser screamed and shouted at us all the way out of the heads. Then the owner of the boat said, 'I normally stay about two kilometres off. I like to stay in vision of the land.'

Fraser told him, 'Well, that's what everybody does. That's why we're going outside so none of those idiots run into us. And if you get it out to the continental shelf, the current is running north. We don't want to fight it. The less time this takes us, the less time we're at sea. The less time we're at sea, the safer we are.'

Fraser's aphorisms have always stayed with me.

The owner got off in Mooloolaba, on Queensland's Sunshine Coast. Fraser had lined up a deckhand-slash-chef for the final few days. What I realised when she got on was that it was adrenaline that had kept me going until Queensland. I'd never done shifts of three hours on, four hours off before. As part of my duties, I had to cook one meal a day. I have no interest, or much experience, in preparing food. My meals were basic and so badly proportioned I didn't get to eat a lot of food. But when this chef got on the boat, her first priority was nutrition.

We picked up a dolphinfish off Fraser Island and over the next couple of nights, it was served as a curry or with vegetables. That nutrition lifted me to another level. My brain was starting to work as it should. I could remember coordinates and my senses sharpened. When we'd get fifteen miles off a coast, I could smell it. I was sleeping better and I was sailing better.

Just as Fraser's words have stayed with me, so has this lesson. If you sail, you're making decisions that are crucial to your survival so you need great nourishment.

Fraser is a man who loves to use his brain. He loves to test it all the time and he has this belief, which I subscribe to, that in the modern world we don't use our brains enough. That's why I have my left-hand days and my right-hand days.

Today, for instance, is my left side. I put my wallet into my pocket with my left hand. I brush my teeth with my left hand. I brush my hair with my left hand. I take the money out of my wallet with my left hand. Tomorrow I'll do the opposite.

All to keep my brain working. So many times in my life I would be heading into the city to pay a bill and next minute I'd be on the Spit Bridge on the way to one of my jobs. As Fraser told me, that's because I don't need my brain to drive.

We live in world where you jump in a car, punch the address into your GPS or your phone, and without thinking you're pulling up out the front of your destination. Because of Fraser, I have a quick look at the GPS, think, I've gotta go up Canterbury Road, take a left on Belmore Road, right through to Picnic Point or whatever. I drive off my own directions. That happens on so many levels, from cooking to cleaning or whatever else it is. You go into auto-pilot and your brain dulls.

That's what I saw in the hospice where Mum died. All these people with dementia who had no clue. They'd lost their brains. I'm a functioning, intelligent human who can build, design and talk to clients but I was letting my brain weaken. Fraser would do everything he could without technology to keep his brain active. Charts instead of GPS. Turning the engine off so he'd be forced to search for the wind.

Fraser likes to average five or so knots an hour. The maths is simple. Every twenty nautical miles is going to take four hours. So if you can nominate where you are in the world, and land is ten hours away, you can realistically go to sleep because you're not going to hit land. But if you're sailing up the coast only ten nautical miles out to sea, you've got to know your position.

All the way up the east coast of Australia there are lighthouses and every lighthouse has a different light sequence: three short flashes, a long flash, two long flashes and so on. We'd be outside Newcastle and Fraser would say, 'What's that light over there, what's the sequence of it?' And I'd study it and say, for instance, 'Three short flashes and three long flashes,' and he would draw a line on the map and we would look at something further up and draw another line and then that's where we are. He'd say, 'In three hours you'll see the lighthouse of so and so, it says here on the chart you can see the lighthouse from twenty miles out to sea. It's two long flashes, a short flash, three long flashes and a short flash. You're going to start looking for that. If you head north-north-east at 365 degrees, for three hours, you want to start seeing that lighthouse.'

Which makes sense, right?

Then we'd go up on deck, I'd take the helm and he'd ask me the sequence of the Newcastle lighthouse. And I would not have a fucking clue. I could not retain that information. I hadn't sharpened my brain enough.

Friends of mine, they'll ring up and say, 'What's your address again? I need to tap it into the GPS.' They've been here ten times and they have to ask the address. I'll say, 'Which way did you come, Bondi Road?' And they'll reply, 'Oh I just followed the GPS.'

In contrast to drivers using their GPS is the motorbike rider. Brendan Jones, Jonesy, is Amanda Keller's radio partner and he rides bikes. He'd been to my house once. Yesterday he arrived out of the blue to say g'day. He didn't have the address written down but he'd … remembered. You have to concentrate when you ride a bike and not just because every second car keeps a one-inch margin between you and death.

After ten days on that first trip to Hamilton Island, when I got off I had the wobbles so bad I fell over in the shower.

On another early trip, this time to Middle Percy Island, we are out to sea, forty k's off the coast. It's morning and I've been on watch from six a.m. It's already hot and the calmest, most beautiful day you could imagine. Smooth seas and not a cloud in the sky. We're the only things on earth.

Then Fraser comes up from below where he's been asleep. He'd do that. In bad weather, he wouldn't sleep for days but when it was quiet, he'd catch up on his sleep.

So he looks to the horizon, does a 360, look around again, says 'Yeah' to himself, looks at his watch, looks up at the sky and says, 'If I'm not awake before five this arvo, put a couple of reefs in the main, strap everything down and make sure the life jackets are on the deck.'

Then he climbs back down to bed.

What the fuck has he just seen?

All day the conditions remain the same. It's beautiful sailing, a ten-to-fifteen-knot wind, we maintain seven knots with no engine, and dolphins and whales share the ride. The occasional bird glides beside us, going off the vortex of the sail.

I say to the other crew member, a young bloke, 'I don't know what Fraser spotted but I think he's got it wrong this time.'

We have lunch. It's a perfect day.

Still, around four, even though I still can't see what he's talking about, I tell the young bloke to put a reef in the sail. He complains that it's such good sailing we'd be mad to put in a reef. I say, 'Nah, put it in.'

I know that if Fraser comes up and we haven't reefed the sail he's going to abuse us. I also know that if he comes up and the weather is beautiful and we've reefed the sail he's going to abuse us. Simple as that.

We tie everything down. We prep the lifejackets. We tidy a few things up.

Well, at five on the dot, this grey, monstrous cloud appears on the horizon. It goes from hot to cold within twenty minutes as the wind whips up to forty knots. To get a boat ready for a storm in good weather takes about three quarters of an hour. In bad conditions it's not only five hundred percent more dangerous but it takes twice as long. If the sails are fully up and don't have any reefs – or knots – in them to reduce the sail area, you're going to be almost touching the water as the boat is pushed over by the wind. And to be able to bring that sail in, the boat has to turn into the wind and face the heavy seas.

Fraser comes up eventually and we sail through the wild night and land at Middle Percy. Later, I pull him aside and I say, 'Listen, Fraser, I gotta ask you a question. You know when you came up from below and you looked at the horizon, well, I'd scanned the sky and there was no evidence of … anything … out there.'

'Wasn't there, you big, useless bastard,' he says sarcastically.

'If there was, I couldn't see it.'

And he says, 'What time did I come up on deck?'

'Dunno, around nine.'

'It was a quarter past nine on the dot. You know what that means, you idiot?'

'No …'

'The weather report was at nine.'

So he'd just listened to the weather report, climbed up, did a little theatrical weather check and then told us what the Met Bureau had just said.

Over our years together, Fraser hooked me on the challenge and thrill of sailing. We did over 15,000 nautical miles together. Drifting to Hobart, Darwin, all over Queensland.

And we delivered four race boats from Hobart back to Sydney.

It ain't a bad record for an amateur sailor like me.

Ah.

Did I mention the one delivery that nearly killed us?

———

A few years after meeting Fraser, he asked me to help bring a beautiful 43-foot steel boat back from the Sydney to Hobart race. He was under a bit of a time constraint because he needed to sail a few of 'em back. He wanted a good crew and he knew he could rely on me. I had drifted with Fraser for a while but my back was still giving me a lot of trouble.

I'd decided that I wanted to walk the Kokoda Trail the following year and people had told me I'd better start training for it. I said that was bullshit and that the soldiers hadn't trained. They were dropped there and they achieved it. And that was how I was going to do it.

A good, long drift with Fraser would do my back good. There's a lot of stretching for ropes and, as it happened, I was looking at buying my own boat and this particular 43-footer with a saloon deck was the sort of boat I was looking for. I was keen to get on it. And Fraser knew it.

There were five of us all up and we flew into Hobart on a grey old night. There was a big swell running with strong winds. We spent the night in a pub and had a few beers. Fraser was never far from a cigarette and a drink at any time of the day.

Despite the conditions, Fraser told us we were heading off in the morning.

'If it doesn't calm down we can stop,' he said. 'But I think this front's going to go through and we'll follow it and we'll get the wind.'

A great sailor wants that wind. You just don't want to be stuck in the middle of it.

We took off from Hobart and the seas were huge. It was awful. The other three blokes on board quickly got violently ill and were incapacitated by the time we moved off the coast. One guy wanted to get off but Fraser wasn't pulling in. We'd been on the boat for twenty-four hours before we even got to the top of the Tasmanian coast.

Now, when you're delivering a boat, if there are five blokes, you divide it so you have two hours on and four hours off. You have to get yourself into a routine of working for two hours and sleeping or resting for four hours. Working for four hours, sleeping for two, working for two, sleeping for four.

Fraser would work out a routine, and then in your routine, you might be preparing a meal or something for the other guys. Fraser always had a really good sequence for that sort of thing. Losing three guys out of a five-guy team early put a lot of pressure on us. It was treacherous. It was a tough sail. The waves were twenty-to-thirty feet and the winds upwards of thirty-five knots.

This is a moment in my life that has really affected me. The image of this lives with me. It still gives me nightmares. We were, literally, in the middle of Bass Strait. We'd lost the engine several times because the seas were so rough and the fuel filter kept clogging up. Although it was freezing, the water in Bass Strait is curiously warm, a contrast to the horribly cold wind. You had to wear goggles and lash yourself onto the helm. Waves would float you as you stood at the helm. Fraser, meanwhile, was either steering or working on the engine in this torrid sea, replacing the filters just so we could have some power for the batteries and for the lights. He didn't sleep.

We just had a storm jib out the front, a small sail. We had the mainsail lashed into all the reefs we could possibly have. Which means it does a few things – it steadies the boat so you're not rocking back and forth, it gives direction, keeps you going where you want to go, and gives you a little bit of control to negotiate each wave.

Here's a thing that's so simple but sometimes hard to comprehend. Waves don't stop. You can't turn them off. Even if it's a fucked day, like this, you can't turn them off. When you sail you do things like breaking down the mathematics of the situation. Okay, the waves are forty-five seconds apart. That means I'm steering through seventy-five waves an hour.

I'd been going for twenty-four hours.

Now, I want you to picture this. I'm in a 43-foot boat with a mast that's fifty-feet high. When we were in the belly of the wave between two great masses of water higher than the mast, it was still and quiet. At the top of that same wave, the boat was laid over, nearly touching the water. That was a monotonous episode that went on for hour after hour after hour, after twenty-four hours, after forty-eight hours. Then you'd go below and try and sleep thinking that each wave was going to capsize the boat and drown you.

Fraser had said to me, 'We're in the main shipping lane, so every hour, make sure you do a full 360° look-out. Just release the helm and turn completely around because there's no way on earth those ships can see us in this. Our radar isn't on. We can't see and we haven't got the power for it.'

I'd been at the helm for about six hours straight and I had floated in every wave that had broken over the boat. By now the waves were forty feet. You would see the next one coming and it would look even bigger. You'd crash down the back of it and then it'd go quiet. The boat would churn to the top, the last eight foot of white water would crash over my face, and I'd hold on for death. I'd see that it was just another drop.

And drop after drop.

I kept thinking, 'How long until I get a break? I can't take much more of this. I'm exhausted. I haven't slept for forty-eight hours. I'm saturated. I'm freezing cold. I'm hungry. I've had enough. I want to go home. I don't want this any more.'

Sailing's taught me that you can't turn life off. You can't. It doesn't stop turning. What happened next was Fraser came through the companionway onto the deck to relieve me. He is the coolest, calmest character I know under pressure, but his face had a look of fear I had never seen. I saw Fraser's face turn white. There was a look of horror I'd never seen before. He was looking behind me. We were sailing into the waves so it wasn't a wave that was scaring him.

As I turned around I could see the rust spots on a tanker that was right behind us. It must've been bearing down on us for a long time. It was about twenty metres off our stern. It was wider than we were long.

It just missed us.

Clearly, the tanker's skipper didn't see us. He was probably asleep at the helm. Or the wind was so loud that he'd sounded the horn but we couldn't see it. Fraser jumped up, grabbed the wheel and steered us hard to port. I'll never forget seeing all those rust spots in the hull and the stench of diesel as it passed my face.

Fraser told me to go below and get some rest. I'd had enough. I lay down in my bunk and sobbed. I fell asleep with exhaustion and woke up with the sun on my chest and the smell of freshly cooked prawns.

I was in the South Coast town of Eden. Fraser had let me sleep and had sailed the boat across Bass Strait alone. It was a beautiful, sunny day and the fishermen were cooking the prawns that they were selling on the jetty there. I got up, stretched and said to myself there was no way I was getting back on the boat.

But I did. I went for a walk through the little town. I saw the museum and read stories of sailors and fishermen, ate some prawns and had a beer in the local club. Got back in the boat and did it all again.

The sunshine on my skin and the warmth gave me a little bit of movement in my back. I was like a flower, I guess. It gets the sun and opens up again. At night it closes down. I learned that night that you have to be prepared. When I got home, I said, 'I'm not doing Kokoda.' My back wouldn't have taken it. I would let people down because I might have to give up. I gave up on the boat that night and Fraser, far more spirited than me, realised that.

People say I've had a few curses what with the second round of cancer, but I reckon that was the closest time I've ever come to death. To see the size, to feel the enormity of that ship beside us was amazing. It reminded me, again, of how insignificant we are in the world. It's up to you to make a mark.

I don't believe in much but I believe that boat wasn't meant to hit us. I believe there's something out there. But I'm a realist too. Although I believe in luck, I do believe that you make your luck as well. I fought every single wave in that journey. The way that the wind was just waiting for us at the top of every wave to knock us over, to knock us down every single time. You can give up if you like, but that doesn't mean it's over. That doesn't mean someone says, 'Okay, wave, stop. He's had enough.'

No. No.

That gives you constitution. I think a lot about that. It must've been like that for soldiers in the war when the bullets didn't stop coming. You want it to be over, but you can't do a damn thing.

It's these adversities that give us the strength to take on things that are bigger and harder next time. This is why I love my life.

I've faced a lot of them.

The bigger the problem, the bigger the adventure.

9
THE HORDERN PAVILION BOAT SHOW 1968–75

It's difficult to overstate the lasting impact the Hordern Pavilion Boat Show had on me and my family. For seven straight years, from the time I was eight until I was fifteen, we saved up and went to Moore Park in Sydney for the Hordern Pavilion Boat Show. Sitting in trailer-sailers that we dreamed of owning were some of the happiest times of my life.

My brother and I would drive up and down the Georges River in our little tinny and vowed that one day we would put a cabin on it and we'd go around Australia, surfing, fishing and living off the land.

It was this simple life that I craved.

Years later, in 2007, Dad was still struggling with the loss of Mum. He couldn't find direction. His dad was French, hence Du Bois, but Dad was the typical

Australian blue-collar worker who never travelled and thought, 'Why would you go anywhere in the world but Sussex Inlet?' There was no better place.

As for France, where half of his family line came from? Anyone who went anywhere else was just a fool and why would you want to go where all those Frogs (as we called them back then) were anyway? That was his attitude.

I'd been looking at boats online for a long time and I decided that a boat was going to give me some happiness. Leonie didn't want to know about boats. But, typically, she supported me, saying, 'Babe, whatever you've got to do to be happy I'll support.'

Leonie's continued support of me got frustrating at times. It seemed I could do no wrong to her. I treated her terribly and she just put up with me. Primarily, because she knew that I was a sick person, a depressed person. What kept me solid at one level was my business acumen. And when everyone was buying property and shares in 2006 and, 2007, I was selling everything. I was that confident I bet against everybody else.

… And buying a boat …

I bought a fifty-foot Beneteau at the Paris boat show in 2006. I took my dad there to be with me when I signed the deal, and showed Dad the Paris that I had fallen in love with.

We looked at the display boat I was buying, we took our socks off and Dad and I sat proudly in it.

Just like we did at the Hordern Pavilion Boat Show, every year from 1968 until 1975.

And he cried. He was filled with pride.

Because for simple people those achievements that you dreamt about as a kid, they're big moments in life. And I saw joy in Dad's face for a long time.

After the Paris boat show, we went to the Beneteau factory at Saint-Gilles-Croix-de-Vie. We saw the hull being formed. Dad was fascinated, proud, excited.

One year later, in 2007, I took Dad back over to Antibes in the south of France where I'd rented an apartment for three months. The boat arrived on a truck at

BARRY DU BOIS & MIGUEL MAESTRE

Antibes and we were going to orientate ourselves with the boat and then head off somewhere. I deliberately booked the apartment about a kilometre-and-a-half out of Antibes, specifically so Dad and I would have to walk into the marina every morning. Dad was loving it. Back in Australia, he wouldn't walk from the lounge room to the dining room; he'd get in his electric car to do it.

We used to joke that his dog was the fattest dog in the street because he went on the electric car everywhere with Dad. My dad was strong as an ox but an unhealthy man. He always had a couple of beers at night and he was a smoker. By that time, he was ninety percent blind as well. But he took to Europe like a fish to water. Dad's a socialist. He was a working-class man and he believed in the worker, and the French are very much like that. They believe the government is a servant to them and not vice-versa.

That's why Dad expected and why I expect more from our government. It's supposed to be a service for us. The hierarchy and the bureaucracy are there for us. I believe that. I believe in the modern day combination of socialist human policies and capitalist economic policies.

Every day we'd walk down to the marina and watch the boat being fitted out.

We'd go to the Carrefour supermarket and buy our crockery and our placemats and everything else we needed.

We finally launched the boat at the end of July 2007. I was the captain of a big, beautiful yacht, the best boat in the harbour in our opinion. Leonie hadn't come over yet but Dad said I had to bring my sister Liz to Antibes.

'She has to see this,' he said.

A good mate of mine, Justin, also joined us, and we started with short sails from Antibes down to Cannes (the famous film festival was on), from Cannes down to Nice and so on.

But Dad was itching to get off the coast. He wanted to go … sailing. This is a bloke who's ninety percent blind. But keen as mustard.

Our first trip was going to be to Corsica. I'd planned it for two weeks. I'd watched the weather maps. The winds around eleven in the evening, when the earth temperature starts to match the sea temperature, turn offshore and we were coming into a full moon. I told Juzzy and Liz that I'd emptied the toilet, I'd paid the harbour master, I'd checked us out and we were going. Tonight. But not to tell Dad. We'd surprise him.

We were at dinner and Dad, like he'd done for the last week or so, said, 'When are we getting the bloody hell out of here? When's it going to happen?'

He had all the bravado in the world.

And I said, 'Well, it's nine o'clock, what about we head off at eleven?'

'You can't do that!' said Dad.

'We can do anything we want.'

'Where will we go?'

'How about we see which way the wind is going and we go with that?'

'Ohhhh, I can't believe it,' said Dad. 'We're going to do it!'

It was one of the most beautiful sails I've ever had. It was the first time I'd been on the open sea as master of a vessel. I'd sailed with my mentor Fraser for over 15,000 nautical miles and I knew I was capable. I'd back myself no matter what. I radioed the harbour master and told him we were pulling out of Nice and that we were headed to Corsica, not that he gave a shit about it, but it thrilled my dad.

I wasn't going to take any risks. I had the headsail and mainsail up with a double reef in both to keep the sail area down in case the wind came up and we found ourselves keeling over and having to pull sails down in a storm. I had the motor ticking over just to be confident and have more control.

It was about one o'clock and, with the change in temperature, the winds picked up nicely and I switched the engine off. I was feeling confident and why sail if you're going to leave the motor running? We were under a full moon, we'd lost sight of land and I was looking at a little radar screen heading for an island called Corsica.

The Milky Way was as bright as it could possibly be and with the full moon we could see into the water and the yacht cast a shadow onto the ocean.

I said to Dad, 'We can't be luckier than this.'

LIFE FORCE

There was no noise and the significance of our lives was obvious. You're just a speck in the ocean.

At about three in the morning, a large pod of dolphins joined us. Dad and I stayed up the whole night. We sailed for twelve hours and the dolphins escorted us from Nice all the way to Corsica and to the port of Calvi.

I could've sold the yacht, I could've given it away there and then, and every cent I'd spent would've been worth it.

10
A DOUBLE MIRACLE

It was more than a scream. This was the wretched wail and sobs of a woman on her knees, a woman ruined by the random unfairness of life. And it was a sound I'd become horribly familiar with.

It was our twelfth time pregnant via the IVF program. It was 2005. Mum had died the previous year. Leonie was sixteen weeks down the track. A month of me injecting into her stomach every day to increase the amount of eggs had finally worked. We had been to the obstetrician. We heard the heartbeats of both of our children. Leonie had morning sickness, too. After so many miscarriages you're wary of being optimistic but these were promising signs.

Leonie has ferocious tenacity and we'd kept trying even as she went through miscarriage after miscarriage. We'd wait the required three months and go straight into the next one. Money didn't inhibit us. The doctors in the IVF program, like most professionals, have a great way of making the statistics work for them. We had 'a ninety-eight percent chance of success'. Now, commonsense tells you that, with those sorts of numbers, you couldn't possibly fail after two miscarriages, let alone eleven.

LIFE FORCE

It had all started so beautifully five years earlier. Not a hitch. The first round worked and on the night of my mate's fortieth birthday, in his speech, he announced that Leonie was pregnant and how proud he was, how proud everyone was. I remember the euphoria of having my mate make his special night about us and the love and support we got from everyone. I thought it was a miracle. I told everyone, 'Go and see an IVF doctor, it works! They showed us the statistics and we're going to have a baby, they guarantee it!' You become this spokesperson for them. By the time you have your second or third miscarriage you start keeping it to yourself. You don't say, 'This is fucked' or 'This is wrong.' You're a little bit scared, you're a little bit hurt and you don't share the information.

In hindsight, I believe we should have. We should share the failures. I believe if we did, others might be more likely to try other avenues of having children first.

I also believe, wittingly or unwittingly, the IVF program, which isn't cheap, plays on your emotions, on your desperation and your hope. No one can understand, can really understand, what it's like to have hope replaced by horror time after time except for the women who so desperately want to give birth to a child. I had given up a couple of times and that formed part of my depression. I didn't believe we were going to have children.

Superficially, life was good, of course. We were living in the North Bondi penthouse and we had everything anyone could want: the sweeping view of Bondi Beach, the cars, the holidays, money, all that stuff.

But when I heard that wail, the crying, I knew straightaway. People don't scream from the toilet and weep in the middle of the night. You just don't hear those sounds in the normal course of your life.

What do you do when the woman you love miscarries, when she loses her two precious children? When your own emotions are scrambled by loss and an instant grief? I tried to console Leonie while I held back how I felt. We went to the hospital that night for a dilation and curette, where the lining of the uterus is scraped out. When you're that far into a pregnancy it's a messy process. They had to give her a curette and from that she got a little infection. And as a result of that happening, we discovered that there were some cancerous cells in her cervix.

Our gynaecologist was a doctor in the reserve army and he'd gone off to serve in Iraq. He saw the results but told us not to worry. When he returned six months later, however, we discovered Leonie did have cervical cancer and that it was well underway.

What that meant was Leonie had to have a radical hysterectomy, as well as have significant glands removed. Because the cancer hadn't spread into her lymph nodes it meant she wouldn't need to have radiotherapy. But it did mean our quest for children, naturally, was over.

It was over.

For me, it was the nail in the coffin of my depression. Euphoria and the heartbreak sank me even deeper into the black. How Leonie survived the miscarriages, the cancer and the radical hysterectomy is beyond me. It shows who the weaker sex is – men.

I didn't handle it at all. I tried to ignore it. I wished it would go away and this nightmare of endless depression and this nightmare of not having children and my wife having cancer would be over. I thought I'd wake up and I'd be back in the perfect world that I'd always imagined would happen.

I didn't know where to go.

One night, I said to Leonie, 'We're not meant to have children.'

She exploded, 'Don't ever say that! That's not the case. We will have children!'

With her lead, we went from IVF straight into adoption. My opinion was it would be a waste of time. Australia has privatised adoption and it's just like any other business. I don't think there's much regard for the children.

But we went through the process. Thousands of dollars were spent so counsellors could come to our house to inspect it, and us, to see if we were fit to be parents. Because Leonie had had cancer she wasn't regarded as a good prospect to adopt even if she was a private trainer – she's the fittest women I know – a nutritionist and, psychologically, has no equal.

We both had to write chronological life histories and because Leonie's dad had left the family when she was little and she grew up without a father figure, it counted against her.

My dad was a drinker and, sometimes, a violent man. But still a great man.

Again, through no fault of our own, this was viewed as a negative. So I was resentful that they thought they were better than us, that these people, most of whom had never had children or the life experiences I'd had, could judge me.

I really rejected it. I'm an arrogant guy, and I was even worse back then, so when they asked for my address and name of my direct superior, I said, 'I've got several addresses and my direct superior is Jesus Christ.'

That didn't go down too well.

It infuriated me. Those judgmental questions. Fuck! Hit me but don't shit me! I remember one of 'em saying they weren't sure about our home. This was when we were living in the eight-million-dollar penthouse on the headland at North Bondi. They weren't sure about the … adequacy … of the joint to raise a child.

I said, 'How about this? If this one's no good, point out the one you think is best and I'll buy that. But don't tell me that my home isn't suitable to raise a child. I grew up in a two-bedroom fibro house on a six-lane highway and I turned out alright. So don't give me the shits. That's all you're doing, annoying me.'

Leonie is smarter than me and she got me to zip it. She knows the only way through bureaucracies is to toe the line and tell them what they want to hear.

It soon became obvious we'd never get a child through adoption in Australia. Five years, ten years, twenty years. It didn't matter how long we waited. It wasn't going to happen. The best we could hope for was to foster and we weren't prepared for the heartache.

Adoption in China was the next option. It would be, naturally, a little girl, the apparent detritus of the state's one-child policy and a cultural belief of the superiority of boys over girls. We shared the news with our family. My dad, my sister and my brother were all really excited for us.

Leonie and I were sceptical of China in the beginning. I had this view that somehow the children might be stolen. I wanted to go and see the country firsthand and so we spent a month there, looking at the culture, talking to people, to the adoption agencies and to other couples. To me, the one-child policy is very sad but, as people said, if we could help one beautiful little girl …

… wait …

When you announce that you're going to adopt a Chinese girl everyone says you're doing these kids a favour. You're not. Let's face it. You're doing yourself a favour. As a human, it's what I wanted. I wanted to love someone and nurture them and give them a sense of belonging. She was going to do me a favour.

What Leonie and I also wanted to create, and this was another reason why we spent so long in China, was a sense of history for the child. When your children are born you can show photos and tell stories of the history that created them, you meeting your wife, how you fell in love, who their grandparents are and so on. But when you're going to adopt a child from a foreign country, that doesn't exist. And you want them to have at least some sense of their history, of how they came to be your child.

We took my nephew Callum with us because he'd be like her big brother. We wanted to be able to say to our child, these are the outfits we bought for you on our first trip to China. These are the photos of all of us, your mum, your dad and your brother when you came into our lives.

A couple of years later, we were still going to group meetings and it went on and on. At one stage we were told we were two years way from having a baby. There you go. You literally set the date. You can set your watch by it. On this date you will fly to China and pick up your baby. And then you get a letter that says, your number is three years away.

We were number 0742.

When the Beijing Olympics came along, the wait suddenly became ten years. China didn't want these adoptions to taint the Olympics or be seen as some sort of failure of government policy. I didn't want to know about it by then. I was so deep into depression that I'd started to hate the whole Western capitalistic system that had made me rich. None of this money was doing us any good.

Then Leonie discovered surrogacy. She studied how it worked and the various laws around the world pertaining to it. We considered surrogacy in South Africa, Greece, South America and the USA but India had laws that suited us the best.

What laws? In South America your sperm is used to fertilise the egg in a woman which makes her the mother whereas in India it's a donor egg so the woman has no skin, so to speak, in the game. In India, they put the intended mother, which would be Leonie, and the father, me, on the birth certificate. The woman who carries the baby, but has no common genetics with the child, isn't on there.

We headed off to India to study the culture and the people and started corresponding with different doctors there. We were excited. I was now starting to come out my depression. My diet had vastly improved so I was healthier. I'd finally started to share my problems with others and therefore my mental health was on the improve.

I was in a good place. Me and Leonie were settled into the South Bondi house and we were excited to be going down the surrogacy route.

We loved everything about India and I couldn't help but be charmed by the people and become fascinated by the culture. I remember being in our hotel in Mumbai and looking down onto the street at four a.m. and it was packed solid. I said to someone, this is the heartbeat of the world. You can see the veins of blood running through it. The traffic, the people, it never stops. In the middle of it all there'd be a cow walking across the road and into the foyer of this five-star hotel.

We met a Muslim family. And it was funny. I was this capitalist Westerner with a socialist heart and these people, while they weren't by any means the lowest caste, they weren't exactly loaded. I wanted to somehow help them more than just by giving them money. I'd already agreed to educate all their children, something I did for most of our surrogates, no matter whether the surrogacy worked or not.

But I wanted to help the family long-term. I never think a handout is effective. I wanted to invest in them so they could make their lives better for themselves. I wanted to buy two tuk-tuks, which is a great business in India. They cost two thousand dollars US each, which is nothing for me, but it meant the husband of our surrogate could employ someone and make a better life for his family.

He looked at me, smiled, and said thank you very much, but I don't want anything. He didn't want anything in the world from anyone. I said, there had to be something he wanted, that he needed. Again, he looked at me, smiled, kissed my hand, thanked me profusely and said, 'What I want you can't give me.' And all he wanted was to be part of the team that carried a statue four hundred kilometres to Mecca. He was allowed to follow but not carry.

BARRY DU BOIS & MIGUEL MAESTRE

And he was right. I couldn't give him that. It was the first of many profound experiences in India.

Let's break track for a second and talk about donating sperm in India. Now, the joint that does the fertilisation of the egg and so on is a hospital more advanced than anything I've seen in Australia. It's like something out of a science fiction movie, particularly to a man who grew up in Moorebank, with a dad who earned his crust reconditioning lawnmowers.

But where you produce the sperm is in a public hospital. And for most Westerners, let alone someone like me with a cleanliness fetish, dropping a load there is going to be a pretty hard day.

First of all, the hospital is packed. The temperature is forty degrees and there are no air-conditioners, just a few fans slowly moving the thick air and flies around but not much else. And this is the hospital where the poorest, sickest people in Mumbai go. And this is where I'm going to give the sperm that is going to fertilise the eggs that are going to create my children.

Phew.

The only Westerners there are me and a couple of gay guys also on the surrogacy trail. My name gets called and I'm given a paper bag with a plastic container for my deposit inside. The nurse shakes her head happily as she hands it over. Did you know that the shaking of the head is an Indian's way of wishing you well? And I ask her, 'So, is there a motel nearby? A serviced apartment building, maybe?'

She points across this sea of faces to a sign that reads Foreign Sperm Donation. It's the only sign in English. I walk into a filthy cell that is one-and-half metres by one-and-a-half metres. I sit, actually I squat, on the vinyl bench that looks like it hasn't been wiped in a year. I don't want to pull my pants down because I don't want 'em to touch the dirty floor. Above me, there are six flies doing the triangle just below the fan.

In what I believe is a triumph of imagination over repulsion, I successfully make the donation. I walk out of the room, give the gay guys the nod, and hand over the paper bag. This isn't an event where you get maximum volume but I'm too nervous to ask if I've given enough.

The sperm goes straight to the hospital where the fertilisation is going to take place. It's a tight schedule. I have to produce at the exact time when the egg is unfrozen and to suit the surrogate's menstrual cycle.

We had six failed attempts with four surrogates.

Six.

What was interesting was that when I was diagnosed with cancer in 2010 I was advised that if I ever wanted to have children I'd need to have my sperm frozen. The doctors suggested I go over to Westmead Hospital, in western Sydney, to inspect my sperm under this new microscope that was eight hundred times more powerful than anything else in the country. I went out there, did the biz, and found that my sperm, while its motility – the ability to move spontaneously and actively – was good, ninety-five percent were defragmented on the head, which meant that they were never going to hold. The upside of that was at least I had five percent with heads like sledgehammers and with Olympian swimming abilities. As it happened, I didn't need to freeze my sperm, but it was good to know that, if we chose the right tadpoles, we could make a baby.

By now I'd spent so much time with the doctors in India that I couldn't help but notice that while they were great doctors, they weren't tremendous business people. And they'd done so much for me and Leonie, and always with love and kindness, that I wanted to help not so much restructure their business but structure it. I was concerned, one, that sooner or later someone might not take a child and they'd be left to deal with an unwanted kid and, two, they'd be bankrupted by people who went into surrogacy without any means to pay. My business ethic is that you have to pressure people when it comes to the money because if someone can't afford something, that's where things go wrong. I also know that humans overcommit to things they can't follow through on.

With that help came certain privileges in return. I was able to go into the scientific rooms where they selected the sperm and where the fertilisation and conception took place. I sat there in a gown and mask watching my sperm swimming on this giant screen. The magnification is such that among billions of sperm, the doctors were able to isolate the two or three that were capable of bashing into an egg. It's fascinating to be in India, this nation of one-point-four-billion people and to be in a world-class laboratory and part of the selection process for the sperm. And then looking through the microscope at the egg, the cell we're hoping to turn into two cells which will turn into four cells, which will turn into eight cells, which is the start of life.

On our seventh attempt, we selected the sperm and inserted it into the cell. And I watched it happen. Back in 2004, I was holding my mum's hand when they turned off the life support and she died, which meant her brain had stopped reproducing cells. It's over.

Seven years later, I'm watching the creation of life.

I want you to picture my day.

It was a hot Mumbai morning. I went to the public hospital and deposited the sperm. We went to the science lab, selected the most athletic of my sperm and put it into the egg. We did that to four eggs. Nothing happened straightaway. The sperm was in there and it was trying to eat and bash its way into the wall of the egg. I was in awe of the science and the pristine nature of this lab. It was world-class everything.

And what happened was I went sightseeing to kill a few hours. I went down to the Mithi River and watched the hotel workers cleaning white sheets in the dirty water. It's fascinating how this works. I had gone from a spotless lab to a river where hotel workers cleaned white sheets in the filthiest water, beating 'em to create oxygenation. A miracle of sorts.

Fifteen hours later, I was back in the lab. I was there, watching, when I saw the cell, the single cell of one of my children go … blip … into two cells. I saw that happen with my own eyes.

I was there for the creation of life. I sat around for hours afterwards but nothing else happened. I was exhausted and in awe. I knew this was the time. I knew they were my children. Right there and then.

And then something happened to me that couldn't happen to anybody else on this earth. I left the hospital, jumped in a taxi and, just as I was about to text Leonie to tell her what had happened, that I was convinced this was it, I started thinking about my day and about my life. I recalled the day Mum took her last breath; I thought about the day Dad passed away. For a powerful moment, I felt they were there with me. And as I had this feeling, as the car pulled out onto this eight-lane highway, the headlight of a car on the opposite side of the road illuminated a bridge over the expressway. And under this bridge were one hundred or so men, women and children asleep on sacks and boxes next to one freshwater tap. It was a sea of motionless bodies.

Talk about a day of contrasts. It was one a.m. and I'd just left a dazzling, high-tech laboratory where I was privy to the miracle of life only to see … *this*. I felt lost. Completely lost.

I had to talk to someone. When I got back to the hotel I told the concierge that I wanted to fix the situation. I wanted to see to it that none of those people were sleeping there the next night. The guy was so calm with me. He said, 'You don't understand, they're happy people. While that's where they sleep, that's where they are and they're happy. They have love and they have family.'

That wasn't enough for me. I convinced him to take me there in the morning. I wanted to save them with money. I'd unholster the old money gun and fire that damn thing everywhere. When we got there, the kids were spraying a hose at each other and running around and laughing in the field next to the bridge. The bridge was just where they slept. The adults worked in a huge market garden.

The concierge talked to some of the men and women of the group. I'd taken lollies, the universal gift to children, but I really did want to save them. I figured I'd buy ten tuk-tuks and get these guys out of poverty. What was that going to cost me, twenty grand? A lot of money, sure, but I could afford it. What if a small sacrifice on my behalf saved a whole community?

But they were happy. While it was a horrific sight that I saw, what they wanted, they said to me, if it was at all possible … if it was at all possible … was a cricket set. You don't need me to tell you that the Indians are cricket mad. And the haircut I was sporting at the time made me look a little like Glenn McGrath, a massive star there. They kept saying, 'Mr McGrath! Mr McGrath!'

I bought a couple of Gray-Nicolls bats and a few balls. Every time I passed that bridge I would see all the kids, and the adults when they weren't working in the field, playing cricket. Screaming and laughing. Smiles for miles.

How can a human, a mere man like me, have all those things happen to him in one day? To see my sperm injected into an egg, to see that cell multiply and turn into what would be one of my children, to have the overwhelming feeling that my parents were with me and to see happiness in the face of terrible poverty?

Nine months later, Bennett and Arabella were born.

You don't leave anything to chance when you've got newborn twins and you're about to fly the coop from the country they were born in. We had a three-hundred-page document that had been photocopied four times, along with the children's blood tests, DNA tests and their results. To get the passports for the kids we were told to send the documents to Delhi.

That wasn't going to happen. I wasn't going to risk a thing.

So I jump on a plane with the documents and with the DNA test that proved Bennet and Arabella were ours. That's twelve-hundred pages of documents in my satchel, along with my underwear and a toothbrush, driving through the slums of Delhi trying to find the Australian embassy.

I get to the embassy and it's cash only. No credit cards accepted and forget even asking about EFTPOS. By this time, the banks are closed and I have to stay the night. The second we get the passports it's straight to the visa office – Bennett and Arabella will automatically become illegal immigrants the second they get Aussie passports – and then we're out of there.

I don't want to waste a second.

The next morning the embassy staff smile and tell me it's a one-week turnaround on the passports and that they'll ring me when it's ready. I say I've got nothing else to do in Delhi so how about I just sit here until it's done? They say to me, well, it could be a whole day. It's a significant discount from the one week initially quoted. I take it.

After the passports came the travails of getting the visas. Now it's hard not to be germaphobic in India. It's just the way it is and the way I am. A billion-plus people mean you're always touching someone. The photographer comes to shoot the visa photos of the kids. To make them open his eyes he blows on their little faces. All I can think about is, 'Stop breathing on my precious babies' faces!' I was also adamant that Bennett was to be circumcised like his dad. But when the doctors asked if I still wanted to go through with it I said, 'You're not going anywhere near him with that knife.' For a man who loves India and its people, it's odd behaviour, I know.

The visa office is like most around the world. There's no way of getting around the system. There are no favourites. You have your documents. You line up. You wait. It's first in best dressed and it's a fucking nightmare.

The office opened at seven a.m. I wanted to be on a three p.m. flight back to Australia so I was determined to get there before anyone else. The limo I was in could only go so far up the road and I could see that the crowd was already starting to form. It was six-thirty in the morning, stinking hot, torrential rain and I ran down this little road, holding a baby in a bag in each hand. There were all these ladies trying to touch the babies and my germaphobia had really kicked in and all I could think was, 'Don't touch them, please don't touch them.' Which is a terrible thing to think, right?

I found a place at the front of the line and waited.

Eventually, the big wooden entry door swung open and a guy came running down the stairs holding two big boxes, the same size as the bags I was holding the kids in. They were both full of screeching masses of rats, the rodents that he'd catch and remove every night before the visa office opened. He was trying to push past me and I was holding the kids and everyone was surging through the door and all the women were trying to touch and kiss the babies as they came past.

I thought, screw this.

I leapt up the stairs, three at a time, holding my two precious bags above the heads of all the Indians and … bang … there I was at the counter.

First one there. It was exactly one minute past seven a.m.

Six hours later, we were heading home.

LIFE FORCE

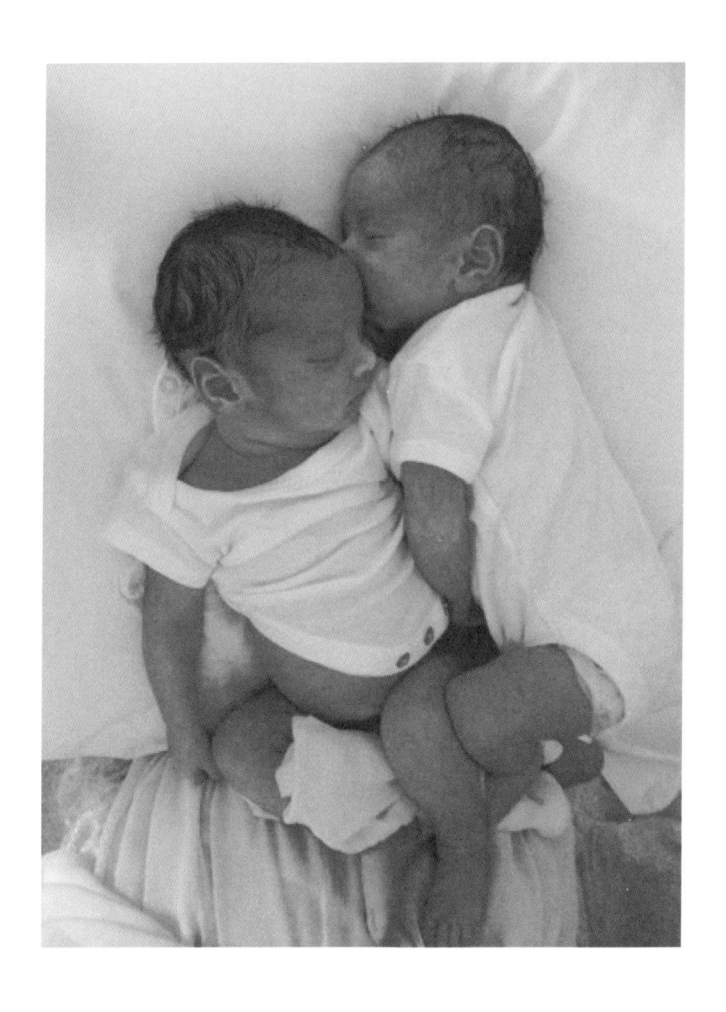

11
MY FIRST CANCER

After the trip with Dad, I joined Leonie for the wedding of a friend of ours in Paris while Mick and Juzzy sailed the boat to Naples.

After the wedding, Leonie and I flew to Naples where we spent two months on the boat together. From Procida on to Ischia, Ponza and Positano, Leonie fell in love with boat life as well. Before she was supportive of me and the boat, but now … now… she had seen, felt, smelt the beauty of sailing in Italy.

When she left to fly home, I was suddenly without a crew and the boat was homeless for the winter. A lot of the talk among the sailors was that Tunisia, in North Africa, was a great place for winter on a boat. The people were sophisticated, it was inexpensive and it was warm all year round.

All I had to do was get it there.

There was some so-called terrorist action in Tunisia, American bullshit in my opinion, and the general consensus was it was too unsafe to go.

Well. I believe if you smile at a bloke when you walk up to him and give him a firm handshake, you're on a level playing field from there. What can happen?

Another friend of mine, Pete Colqhoun, is a passionate architect and he loves to travel. He's passionate about the built environment and what it does for humans (think: *The Architecture of Happiness*). Being a lover of design, a world traveller and a well-read man makes him a great partner for me. And he feels secure that I can get us anywhere. It's a great combination. I'm the rough diamond and he's the articulate one. I love our friendship dearly.

Pete was on TV and short on time, but he loved a trip. He had a partner who'd let him go at the drop of a hat, but Pete always came with the mind that, somehow, he could turn our trip into a documentary or some kind of TV show.

I rang him.

'Where are you?' he said. 'I'm keen as mustard to see you!'

I told him I was in Italy and I wanted to go to Tunisia and that the other blokes had dropped out because they were scared of terrorists. I knew Pete would go anywhere so I told him to fly to Sicily and we'd take the two-night sail down to Tunis together, maybe even traverse along the Libyan coast.

Pete said he'd love to go to Tunisia but he didn't have the time for the sail. Could I get down there without him?

'Give me a day and a time and I'll be waiting at the dock,' said Pete.

What the hell, I'd sail singlehandedly from Sicily to Tunisia. I did some rough calculations with the weather and my ability, gave Pete a date and off I went.

On a solo crossing, you sleep a couple of hours on, a couple of hours off. I had all the radar, all the modern technology, so if something came within my range, if it looked like there was going to be a collision, an alarm would wake me up. I'm a careful and considered sailor, my wind pattern was good, and I figured: I've sailed all over the world with Fraser, I'm going to be okay in the Med.

I didn't tell Leonie I was going to Tunisia. I only told Pete. Into the second night, I hadn't spoken to a single person and I started to question and analyse my decisions.

I thought, what if something goes wrong here? This would be an interesting way to go. No one would know. No one would have the boat to play with because I'd be gone and the Tunisians would probably sink it or whatever and the media

BARRY DU BOIS & MIGUEL MAESTRE

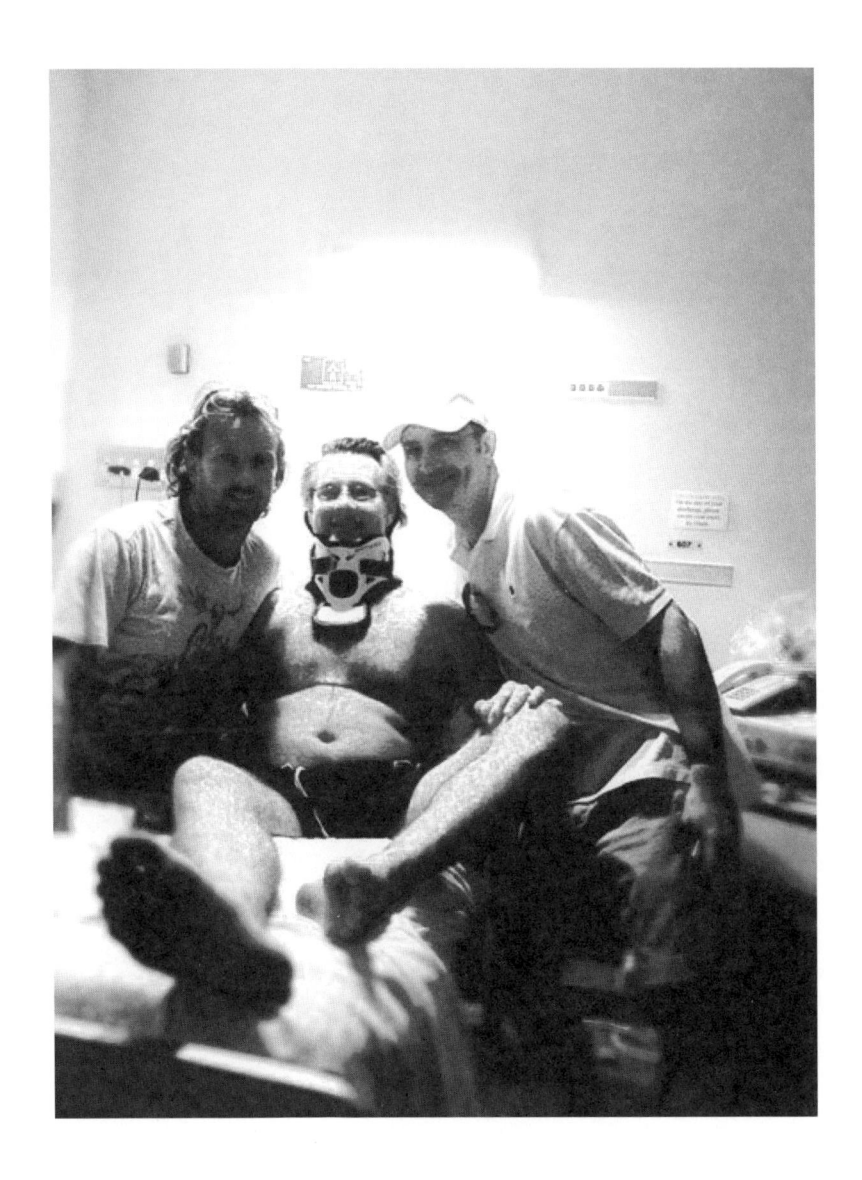

would put out a bullshit story about terrorism. I love to question my decision making, think of ways to be sharper, but out in the middle of the sea on a dark night, it can really put the wind up you.

I didn't fall overboard; I didn't have a heart attack. And the arrival of a red ball sun at dawn quickly evaporated my doubts.

I've got a rule that I always like to arrive at a port around nine or ten o'clock in the morning. And definitely no later than lunchtime. Because in the late afternoon and places are full, people are starting to get cranky. I like to arrive at that time in the day when people will welcome you and then if something goes wrong you've got six or seven hours' lead time to work it out.

I sailed through the day and spotted land as the sun set. Now, the Bay of Tunis is about forty nautical miles from entry to port so that's another seven hours just to get in. And as it happened, I arrived early. I was going to dock at six. I was beyond tired. I was exhausted, mentally and physically. I thought to myself: this joint is thirty times bigger than Botany Bay and not treacherous at all, at least in an oceanic sense, but I don't know it. I don't speak any Arabic and I had just read the pilot book that said, 'Don't mention that you don't have weapons on board 'cause they'll come and get you.'

I trailed the edge of the bay. Ten nautical miles in I saw some nice little sheltered anchorages where I could get a few hours' sleep and still be able to arrive mid-morning. I dropped anchor in six metres of water. There was no moon, no lights but I could see on the maps that I was in a remote area.

I didn't know how safe it was so I left the radar, with a five-hundred-metre protection zone, on overnight. If someone came into my radar, the alarm would go off and I'd come up and see what was going on.

I had a shower and my head had just hit the pillow when the alarm started. I raced up on deck, but couldn't see anything because of the moonless night. I checked the radar and I could see six little boats moving in, hearing the alarm, moving off, coming back in, hearing the alarm and moving off again.

Can you imagine? My brain started to race.

Fuck me.

I'd put my foot in it here. I'd underestimated things. I shortened my radar zone to 250 metres, they kept coming and backing off, coming and backing off. I shortened it down to 125 and still they came.

I wanted to see who it was. I wanted to see if they were coming for me or if they were going somewhere else. Was I in a path here? I was too tired to lift anchor. I wasn't going to move.

One week earlier, I'd dropped anchor over a cable and the coastguard had come and told me to get it off. I couldn't see any cables on the chart. In the back of my mind, I started to think, these bastards were coming to get me.

I had to think about that.

I sat there and watched them come further and further in. Very slowly they came in. It made me suspicious that they were trying to sneak up on me.

When they hit the 125-metre mark, I started to hear Arabic. I didn't say a word. I turned off my navigation lights and my anchor light. Every time they heard the alarm, they backed off. But still they tried to come.

What was going on?

I figured, if it was like that then come and get me. They had come to get the wrong bloke. They might get me in the end but I was going to take a few of 'em out. I was sitting there, in a little bed at the back of the boat, with knives strapped to both thighs and a loaded speargun in my hand, which was incredibly dangerous … to everyone. Next to me was what I call the 'Equaliser', a baseball bat. I come from the western suburbs of Sydney. Baseball bats promise security.

The companionway, the entry to the boat from the sea, is only narrow so I figured they could come but I was going to go down fighting. It was as simple as that.

At about five-thirty, the sun hit my face. I'd fallen asleep with my loaded speargun in my hands. It was lucky I hadn't shot myself. As my eyes cleared, I realised what I had done. I had dropped my anchor in the middle of all these families' fishing nets and they were just trying to get 'em. The alarm scared them more than it scared me. They didn't want to come any closer because they were sensible people. They didn't know what was going on and they didn't want to have a confrontation in the dark.

When I woke, they were holding fish above their head and waving. They had binoculars on me and they could see me asleep with my speargun and knives.

After I'd stood up and peeled off my weapons I turned off the alarm and waved 'em over. They couldn't speak English and I couldn't speak Arabic. We exchanged gifts. They gave me fish. I gave them stuffed koalas and Bondi Beach t-shirts, presents that were useless in every regard.

They embraced me and gave me one water; I apologised, lifted anchor and sailed into the port of Tunis.

Tunisia is a strict Muslim country. Forget about buying a drink, no matter what your thirst is after a few days on a boat. Which ain't such a bad thing. It keeps the weight off, stops a man doing stupid things.

For me, the Islamic architecture, the use of light, the reference to mathematics, stunned me. I could've wandered around Tunis for days marvelling at this beautiful port.

Pete wasn't at the dock but he'd left a message with the harbour master that he was at the airport. I made friends with the guy beside me who'd lived in America and could speak English. He told me I was safe here. I trusted him and he was right.

I caught a cab to the airport. Pete met me, we embraced and I took him to the boat. Now, Pete has been a lifeguard most of his life, he's an incredible ocean man, a surfer, but he gets seasick, bad. The plan was to spend some time in Tunisia, sail back to the Amalfi Coast in Italy and fly home from Naples four weeks later.

But what Pete had done during his thirty-five hours of flying was to research North Africa. Instead of sailing straightaway, we jumped on a plane and flew to the foot of the Atlas Mountains on the border with Libya, where we started a 1200-kilometre trek by camel and four-wheel-drive. Our guide didn't speak English so he taught us Arabic folk songs and we taught him a bit of Slim Dusty.

On that journey, Pete, who was an architect for the TV show *Great Australian*

Sandcastles and *Better Homes and Gardens*, saw our trip as a great opportunity for a show about two blokes from two very different worlds sailing through the sea gates of cities that had changed the world.

Carthage, Tunisia, was one of the epicentres of the world. One of the great early civilisations. It dominated the Med in the thousand years before Christ was born. It was where the great Carthaginian general Hannibal left with his elephants to, eventually, cross the Alps, which was ballsy as hell, and take on the Roman Empire in Italy.

Pete figured we could use the boat to have holidays and make the show at the same time. We'd sail to the city, decode the architecture, film it, sell it. It was going to be called *Cities of the Sea*. It was typical of a couple of larrikins. We'd sail our yacht, pull out a camera and make a TV show.

I wasn't fussed on TV at all. I didn't think I had the head for it. I definitely wasn't articulate enough for it. But I trusted Pete.

I said, 'Do what you like, mate.'

The following year, we went back and sailed for seven weeks, following Homer's Odyssey. We studied the architecture of Syracuse, Palermo, Gozo. We had eighty hours of footage. We interviewed the mayor of Corleone. There was film of me arm-wrestling a giant Sicilian tuna fisherman in Favignana, where they have the tuna killing fields, where sashimi masters choose the fish to put on a jumbo jet that night to go to Japan. At the time, I was well over one hundred kilos and a powerful guy. I rarely got beaten in an arm-wrestle. The bikies at the Sundowner Hotel used to back me in the seventies when I was a skinny kid. I could handle myself when things went wrong. I won the wrestle with the Sicilian fisherman, by the way.

A year later, *The Renovators*, a home improvement game show on Channel Ten, started casting. A friend of Pete's had seen all the footage of us sailing into all these cities. And Pete rang me up and said, 'There's a show coming out on Channel Ten and I reckon you're perfect for it. They want a building mentor.'

I told him, 'Mate, I'm not interested in TV. Look at my life. Six months in Bondi, the rest of the time in Europe. Leonie and I are as happy as we've ever been and we've just started surrogacy. You couldn't pay me enough to leave this.'

He told me to do him a favour and have a talk with them. Pete thought they were going to offer me decent money and, because he does it himself, thinks being on a TV is a great thing.

I didn't. I thought *The Block* had screwed builders. We don't wear khaki every day and put treated pine posts in a hole with ready-mixed concrete. I don't believe you have to be a yobbo to be a builder with your arse hanging out of your pants and drinking twist-tops on the job. That ain't what we do. It ain't what I do.

So Pete made a sizzle reel for the architect role, even though he was Channel Seven through and through and there was no way he was going to Ten, and filled the reel with our journey to Tunisia and Malta. One of the big execs saw it and said, 'The architect's good but that big bloke is perfect as the builder.'

When an executive says you're perfect and they want you, I know now, they're going to get what they want. They got a casting agent to call me. I had just arrived in Istanbul and I was in customs, struggling with everything, and I told 'em I wasn't interested, that Pete shouldn't have given them the number, but thanks for calling.

Shortly after, *Business Review Weekly* called me and asked if they could tell my story. Because even though millions of people had predicted the Global Financial Crisis after the fact, very few people had done anything about it. In the article, I explained that you've gotta run your own race. You can't be a sheep. By doing that, I was now living on this yacht six months of the year and we were about to buy a home in Paris. Calling the GFC before it happened had set me up for life.

The executives had read that and they wanted me even more.

By Christmas 2009, six months before *The Renovators* started, I was back in Australia for Christmas. Mick and I had met at Mum and Dad's place at Sussex Inlet. We'd decided to sell it. It was very hard to let go of but it meant I got to have a surf with my brother.

It was Christmas and I was on a longboard riding across a wave when the opportunity came for an old bloke, me, to duck the head and get a tube. The lip

BARRY DU BOIS & MIGUEL MAESTRE

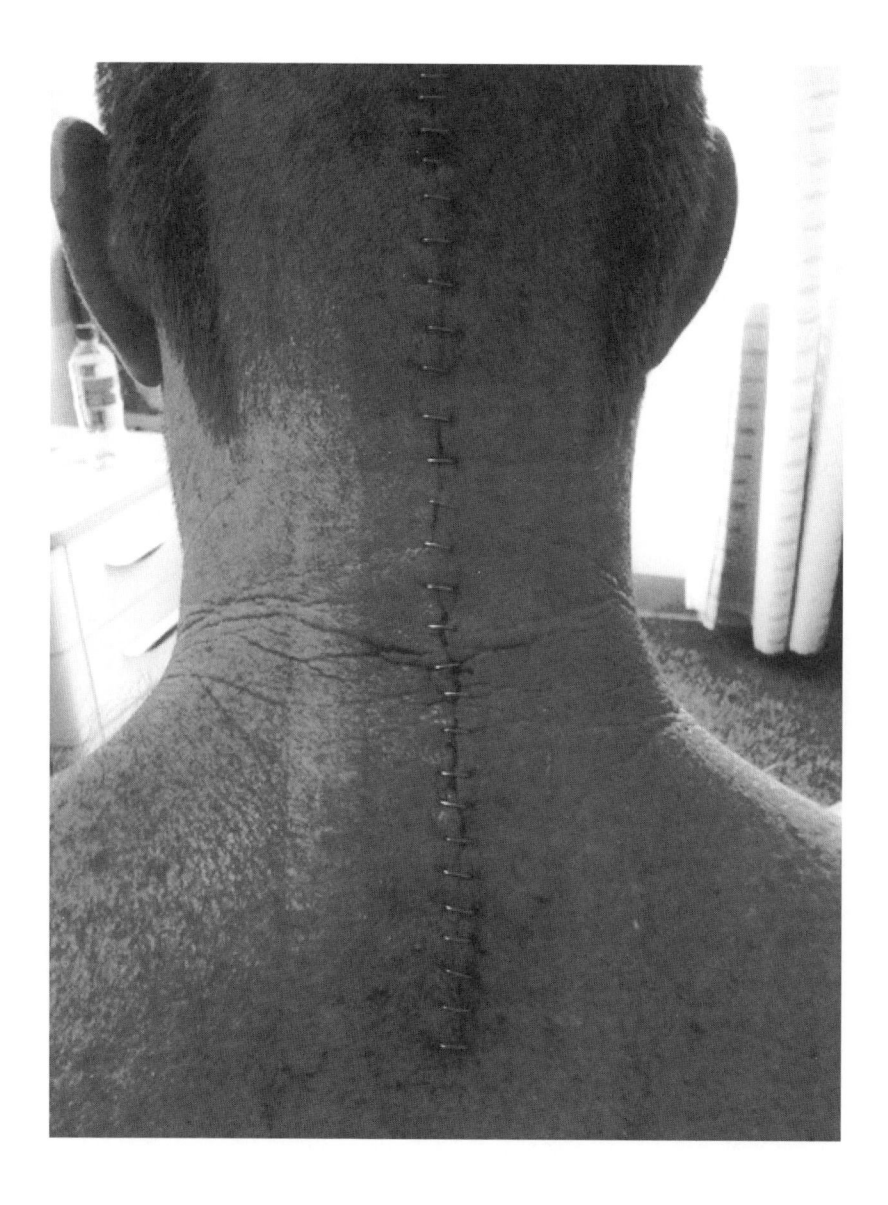

of the wave hit me on the side of the neck and knocked me off the board. The pain was excruciating. It was a pain that started in the head but spread to below my hips. I felt pins and needles in my head. I sensed straightaway that something was very wrong.

I've been hit by enough blokes, been in enough tackles, had enough things fall on my head to know that a wave couldn't have done that much damage. I was confused. But I was also very numb in the water and my brain told me that I couldn't move my neck. I was face down in the water and the next wave washed me closer to shore. I was only underwater for thirty seconds but that's a long time when you can't breathe or move.

I got my footing and straightened my back up and reached for my head. A wave washed over me and it was like being hit with electric shocks all the way to my knees. My toes started to go numb. I knew there was something crucially wrong. I staggered to the shore and sat there holding my head. I couldn't move it at all. I was locked up like a vice.

I said to Mick, who'd come in to see what had happened, 'I don't know what I've done but I've done something to my neck.'

He asked me if I wanted to go to hospital but I brushed it off and said I'd see my chiropractor when I got back to Sydney.

What had happened that day was a giant tumour had eaten away my whole C1 vertebrae. It isn't a big vertebrae but it's the connection for your neck and your skull. It has a little knob in it where the skull sits and it's where your head pivots off, and then there's the ligaments, muscles and tendons around that.

When the wave had hit it, the bone had caved in like an eggshell. The fibre of the tumour, a vein and some muscle were the only things holding my head on.

But I didn't go to the doctor. I don't believe in running off to doctors so I went to my masseuse. I'd broken my back a decade before and it didn't stop me. This was just a sore neck and a bit of a headache.

I booked a trip to India to deposit some sperm for our surrogacy. It was still a couple of months away and I knew my neck would come right by then. But it didn't come right. It settled down but I couldn't move it. My masseuse worked at the Australian Institute of Sport and she put me onto the physiotherapist there.

He said, 'I can't take the risk of touching you. There's more damage than just the tightness of your head. Before we go any further we need a picture of this.' He told me I needed an MRI urgently.

Meanwhile, the casting agent had called two more times. I'd had enough and told 'em never to call me again, but it made them want me even more.

I went to India and the pain was unbearable. The headache would've killed the average man. I'm not joking. I can bear a lot of pain but I couldn't take it. I was dosed up to the eyeball on painkillers, which I hate. Before I'd left for India I'd seen my old doctor and said I wanted a referral for an MRI. He'd already done an X-ray but couldn't see anything. Which amazes me in hindsight. The results would be in the morning I came back from India.

I told Leonie to book me into the physio for three hours because we had to fix this problem. Told her to tell him to bring everyone he needed. I wanted this fixed. I was very impatient. A rude, arrogant bastard, I was. I had plenty of money and not many people told me what to do.

I went into the medical centre in Bondi on my Harley and told the receptionist I was there to pick up my MRI. I was in intense pain and short-tempered. She told me I couldn't just pick it up and that I had to see a doctor.

I said, 'I'm not seeing a doctor. Tell me how much it is and I'll give you the money for my results. I don't care what your doctor says. I'm not interested in what some GP think about my neck. I need this MRI, I paid for the MRI so I wouldn't have this problem, and I'll pay you to give it to me and just let me go.'

And she said, 'No, I can't do it. I'm really sorry. You're going to have to sit down.'

She had the shits with me because I was being a dickhead.

After a while, I said, 'I apologise. I'm really sorry. Can we just make this happen?'

She softened, told me she'd take a look at it and if there was nothing too dramatic, I could grab it and leave.

It was a funny situation because I'd been such a dickhead and had made such a scene. And this woman, to her credit, opened the MRI report and she started to read it. Under her breath, she went, 'Ah, shit' and she said, 'Sorry, you're going to have to see the doctor.'

She gave the report to someone and she grabbed me by the hand. None of this was making sense. I'd been such a dick and she took me by the hand and led me upstairs. The doctor was a Russian woman, middle-aged. She'd read the report by this stage, too. She leant close, so close I felt uncomfortable, put her hand on my leg and asked if I had a family.

I said, 'What's wrong? I've got a bad headache and a sore neck. Just relax. Tell me what's going on. Whatever it is, we'll fix it. Don't worry.'

She said, 'I'm not so sure, Barry. I'm not sure we will. You've got a massive tumour that has eaten your spine and is attacking your brain. I've never seen anything like it.'

I said, 'You've got the wrong MRI. That ain't me. There's nothing wrong with me. Sore neck. Bad headache. That's all.'

It was quiet and I think from that moment, life slowed down. I can recall so much of it, the room, the doctor, the tears in her eyes.

She said, 'You're in a lot of trouble, Barry. I don't know any other way to put it. I want to call an ambulance and have you taken to hospital.'

I told her I wouldn't be going in any ambulance.

She said, 'I can't let you drive. You have a broken neck.'

And then she said, 'I don't know what to do.'

I texted a mate, whose brother was one of the managers at St Vincent's hospital and wrote, 'I have a plasmacytoma, it has eaten C1, C2, attacking brain, who do I see?'

I knew St Vincent's was the best hospital. When Mum and Leonie both got cancer I realised that if you have the means, you don't just take the first bed. You research the best hospital and that's where you go.

He texted me back telling me to ask her for a referral to this particular doctor and that he'd take it from there.

I asked her for the referral and she told me that there was no way this doctor was going to see me without private insurance.

I told her, 'Don't worry about private cover. I'll just pay for it.'

She told me that no one could afford that sort of treatment and that she'd give me a referral for the public system just in case.

I texted my friend and said I had the referral and could he get me an appointment. He hit me straight back: 'I've already spoken to him and he's on a day off but he's going to come and see you. Go to his office. He'll be there at twelve.'

I knew of the doctor. He was the head guy. A big reputation. If I could get him, I'd be in great hands. I rode my bike home to Leonie and told her the news. It was the hardest thing I'd ever done, especially after everything she'd been through and the fact I'd just been to India in our quest for children.

It didn't compute. I felt like a lesser man. This great protector and provider might not have the ability to look after his family. I was scared as shit. There were people crying all around me. I could be leaving. None of this made sense.

I drove to the appointment. The receptionist at a specialist's office is a gatekeeper. She doesn't let people through who can't pay. She asked me what sort of hospital cover I had. I told her I didn't have any.

She said, 'You're not seeing the doctor. You can go through the public system, but you're not seeing him. Can you wait in the foyer over there?'

I said, 'No, he has told me to meet him here at twelve. I'll wait here.'

'Well, you're not allowed to wait here in the office. Can you wait outside?'

I texted my mate, who texted the doctor. I told my mate, if I had to I'd give him money up front if that's what they needed. I was in that position, money-wise. It sickens me that money talks, but when you're on death's door, or think you're knocking, you'll do anything.

The receptionist came over and apologised and let me sit there in the office.

The doctor arrived and he'd read the report. He knew I was in a lot of trouble. He didn't know what he was going to do with me either. In his view, I had a broken neck and I was walking around. I could be paralysed from the neck at any second.

At any second. And it had been three months.

Fuck!

He took me into his office and said, 'Mate, I have no clue what we're going to do here. I've arranged a meeting this afternoon with an oncologist and another surgeon and we'll pull in whatever it takes. What you've got is massive. Which means it's incredibly aggressive. Even if you've only had pain since Christmas this thing is rampant in you. We want to do another MRI. We want to see how much cancer is in you. But it's not good, mate. It's not good.'

In hindsight, I'd put up with this pain for twelve months and the surfing accident was the final straw. Since breaking my back ten years before I'd lived with pain. It isn't an issue for me.

I sat there waiting for him to realise he'd made a mistake and that I just had a crook neck and someone was going to snap it back into place for me.

Later that day, Leonie and I sat down with the three doctors.

One openly said, 'Because of the size and aggressive nature of the tumour, and we'll double check but if we're right, you're full of cancer. You'll have other cancers as well because this is a secondary cancer, which means you're in a lot of trouble. I'm going to estimate three to six months. I suggest you spend as much time as you can with your family.'

My wife said, 'We're not fucking interested in that.' She actually used that profanity.

I looked at the guys and I said, 'I promise you. I'm not going anywhere. I'm not. I'm not ready and I won't let it happen. You do what you can do and I promise I'll do the rest.'

This was a profound moment in my life. Again, the world slowed down. The words came out of my mouth in slow motion. I could see the second-hands on the wall clocks barely moving. By now I was in a neck brace.

The doctor said, 'Baz, you're not going to believe it, but there's a guy in the country at the moment from England and he's one of the only guys in the world I'd trust to do this. I want to put a rod in your neck, get into where the growth is and take a biopsy. But we've gotta navigate past your artery and through the spinal cord.'

I said, 'Mate, I'll do anything. Knock me out and you can cut my head off if you like as long as you glue it back on in the afternoon.'

Here's the kicker. He said, 'No, you've gotta do it all conscious.'

Now, I'm petrified of needles. I'm not scared of much but I'm petrified of needles.

'The problem is I only get one shot,' he said. 'Because if I hit the artery, we can't go through the other side so I'm going to have to open you up. I've gotta do this with you fully conscious because if you stroke out or we paralyse you I need to back off.'

I thought, I need my brother here. I knew he was only a phone call away. I needed to tell him that some idiot had just said I've got three to six months to live. I had some sorting out to do. I still had properties, shares, maybe a little gold in the bottom of the boat.

I turned the phone on and as soon as it lit up, a private number rang. I apologised but the doctor told me to take it.

It was the casting agent. If you've ever been called up by a casting agent you'll know they're comically upbeat. I was in a room where my wife was crying, a doctor had just delivered my death sentence and this voice on the end of the line went, 'Hi Barry! It's Kirsty from Cast of Thousands! I know you told me not to call back but we just want you to know that we will do … anything … to get you in for a casting for this show.'

I stared at the phone for a second and I thought, 'That'll do me. This isn't real.'

I was going to throw the phone out the window but as I looked at it I had the same sort of epiphany I had at the Lord Dudley that night when I chose not to fight.

'I tell you what, Kirsty, I love that you've called me. You call me back in three months and if I answer the phone I'm going to do it.'

And then I hung up. End of story.

For the next nine weeks, I had intensive radiotherapy. Because of my size I'd taken the maximum dose and I'd had major surgery. The photos of the operation are horrific. I'd gone from 115 kilos to 78 kilos. I was in a bad way. All through the treatment I thought about the offer.

And I decided, 'You know what? I'm going to be on TV.'

It gave me strength. I was still sceptical as shit about TV, I still thought it was for dickheads, but if I lived after what I told the casting agent, it had to be a sign.

So I went in for the casting. They'd sent up a scenario for the show. Before I went in, I'd asked Pete what to do and he said, 'Baz, if they want you, they want you.'

I said, 'But I really want it now!'

I arrived in a little GoGet Toyota and out stepped a skinny bloke. Now that confused 'em straightaway.

We're there on set, and remember the market had crashed and property was on the nose, and the executive of the show said, 'What we have here is this couple has bought this house for eight hundred thousand and we're going to give them ten percent of that value to renovate. Because that's the number you go to.'

I said, 'Where did you get that bullshit from?'

'Oh, it's just a formula a lot of the experts tell us.'

'What experts tell you that?'

Because TV people aren't, generally, experts. It's what we tell people to make them buy shit.

'And then they're going to renovate.'

I said, 'What do they do for a living?'

'He's an accountant and she's a secretary.'

'What makes them think they can do it?'

'Well, just imagine, we're going to give them some guidance and you're going to mentor them.'

'Fair enough,' I said. 'I'll have a go at that.'

'And then they're going to sell it and the profit they get to keep.'

'There's no profit in this joint, mate.'

'Well, this place next door is valued at one point two million.'

'I don't care what it's valued at, it's a seven-bedroom place in an area full of four-bedroom homes. It's overcapitalised to the shithouse. And look at this thing. It's covered in Band-Aids and it needs a heart transplant. You're going to spend your eighty stripping back the shit people have put in over the last twenty years. There's some character but it's going to take you a long time to find it.'

He said to me, 'Right. What would you do with eight hundred thousand dollars at the moment?'

'Well, at the moment, I'd put sixty percent in some blue chips, twenty percent in mid-cap companies and I'd leave the rest in the bank because I think there is still another downturn to go. You can pull seven percent in the bank. Better than the market average and if you're doing better than the market average you're doing pretty good. Investing, son, is for the long term.'

I was really me. And I was talking to one of the executives in TV.

'After this,' he said, 'I'd like to talk to you about my portfolio. But let's just go with this scenario for now.'

'Yeah, alright, mate.'

I thought they were all mugs. They didn't have a clue what they were doing. One of the tradies on the show – nearly all the tradies in Sydney have worked for me or someone I know at some point – had rung a mate of mine and the mate rang me and he said, 'Did you just do a casting?'

'I just went to some TV thing. Dunno how I went. None of them know what they're talking about.'

My mate said, 'Fuck, you've impressed them I tell ya! They all think you're a dick but ask for whatever you want because they're raving about ya!'

And, sure enough, six months later, *The Renovators*, co-starring a very green Barry Du Bois, went live. While I was sceptical at the beginning, *The Renovators* team were incredible and the producers taught me so much. It was an incredible learning curve for me and it was great to realise that I could share my knowledge with so many people. I love TV now.

12
A MAN'S GOTTA SING

I love to sing. Boy, I love to sing. If a Diana Ross or Aretha Franklin tune comes on the radio when I'm driving, I'll blow the windows out with my warbling. You know how it is. The road ahead is the audience, the driver's seat is the stage, your fist is the microphone. Tradies and builders know the feeling especially well because we're always burning around town between jobs belting out songs.

Put on 'You Make Me Feel like a (Natural) Woman', 'Respect' or 'You Are Everything' and I'll do my damnedest to hit every single note.

And yet.

I've always been very self-conscious. You won't notice it on the TV, the old fake-it-till-you-make-it maxim has served me well on the box, but it's true. You'll never see me in public without a shirt on, for instance. I worry about how I look to others. I worry about my voice. Do I sound like an idiot? Like a cat being throttled? Does my mouth look weird? Do I contort my face?

Cue: anxiety.

Karaoke is something I'd always wanted to do but fear ruled me. I was just too scared to do it. Wait. More than scared. Mortally terrified.

Back in 2010, I'd flown to Greece to pick up my yacht and sail it to the old port of Syracuse in Sicily with a couple of old friends, Pete and Craig. Both sing. I keep a guitar on my boat and when Pete picks it up and starts a song, I rarely sing along, I just listen. It's something to be a hundred nautical miles off the coast and the only sounds are the slap of water against the hull and a good friend mastering an old soul classic. Craig is a natural on the tonsils. He can write a song, too. Every time he got a new girlfriend, he'd write her a song. Talk about the fastest way to a woman's heart.

Anyway, we decided to use our sails all the way to Sicily. We didn't want to start the engine, not even once. It's a challenge as a yachtsman to use only the wind on a voyage and all of us love to be pushed. We motored through the Corinth Canal, ran into some bad weather and found ourselves a long way south. It took all our skills – how easy it would've been to kick the diesel into duty – but eventually we came into Syracuse on Sicily's south-east coast.

Syracuse is one of my favourite ports. The history. The architecture. Greek ruins and amphitheatres. Cicero called it the greatest of all the ancient Greek cities and its most beautiful. The mathematician Archimedes, the Eureka guy, was born there. And there's a bar Pete and I always visit when we're in town. We told Craig all about it, all the stories. So there was a buzz about going to this joint and liberating it of its liquor stores.

Whenever I'm sailing I've got a bit of a beard, my hair's longer and I'm windswept from being on the yacht. And the guy who owns the bar is an old Sicilian. He doesn't speak one word of English. But he calls me the Sea Wolf. I love that. The fact that he remembers me but also the cool image he has of me. It does wonders for my self-esteem. I'll swing through the door and it's like he's been waiting for me. Orders the drinks. The first round is always on him. Always. Pete will get up and sing with the band. It's a hell of a good time, especially when you've been on a boat for a week looking at nothing but the two weathered faces of your mates.

I told the boys that as soon as we pulled into port we were going to have lunch at this bar and it's where we were going for dinner and drinks. The boys were tired but you gotta eat, right?

As we arrived for lunch we saw a big sign on the door.

KARAOKE TONIGHT.

I hadn't been there for three years but the owner looked at me, opened his arms, beamed like a lighthouse and said, 'Sea Wolf! Sea Wolf!'

Then he smiled and said, 'Karaoke, karaoke.'

I coughed nervously. 'Ah yeah …'

We have one of those classic relationships where neither of us speaks the other's language. We don't talk much. We just smile and nod a lot and bump each other's shoulders. I'm sure he's like that with a lot of people, but I feel we have a connection.

He kept saying, 'You karaoke, you karaoke.'

I was saying, 'Yeah, yeah,' but I had no intention of going near the karaoke machine.

How could I stand up in public and perform karaoke? It was so far out of my comfort zone I couldn't even entertain the idea. But over lunch I thought to myself, you know what? This is something I've always wanted to do. I'm in a bar where no one knows me, not that that should ever worry anybody anyway, but no one knows me. And half the people don't even speak English.

What have I got to lose? Isn't there an aphorism about doing something that scares you every single day? I'm a man's man. A boxer. A sailor. A builder. Surely I can bang out a song.

Pete had always said, 'Whenever you take on karaoke, pick a song that everyone knows so they'll join in, and make it short.' For me, that song was Rodriguez' 'I Wonder'. Great song and only two-and-a-half minutes long.

For the first time in my life, I felt something in me stir. I was going to do karaoke. I had all day to prepare. I'd sung that song a thousand times but I wanted to give my whole self to those words. That's what entertainers do. I wrote all the words to 'I Wonder' out on a sheet of paper. I'm dyslexic so the written words don't exactly … compute … with me, but it's something. Maybe a few lines would sink in.

As I practised, I felt like I should start getting some moves happening. There's a seesaw rhythm to this song and I figured, if I moved, I might be able to keep the tone and the rhythm on track. As I was singing 'I Wonder' over and over, readying for my big debut, I could hear Pete and Craig singing in their wonderful, natural, booming voices, all heart and passion. Sailors in port for one night without a damn care in the world.

I finally told 'em. 'I'm going to do karaoke tonight. I'll have a few beers, I'll loosen up, get on stage and have a go. I won't be able to remember the words but they'll be on the screen so I'll be fine.'

I got a couple of slaps on the back. Yeah, mate. Nice one.

We had a nap. Got up and hosed down the boat. It was nine p.m. Karaoke started at nine-thirty.

We walked to the bar. I was so nervous it was unbelievable. It was like running onto a football field in front of fifty-thousand people. I'd been to the toilet at the marina but I had to go to the toilet again when we got to the bar. I had three beers in short time.

Then, my old pal the owner climbed onto the stage and announced that the first song of the night would be performed by his friend from Australia.

I thought, 'Well, no pressure there.'

And I'm sitting there, going through the words, feeling good, knowing it was going to be perfect. I'd analysed the scenario: a million miles from home. No one gives a shit about it.

Then, 'E ora, il mio grande amico australiano, il lupo del mare, canterà, I Wonder di Rodriguez.'

The music started. The first words came up on the screen. It was in Italian.

I froze. There was nothing in me. I moaned the few English words I could remember into the microphone. There was no booing. No one threw tomatoes or laughed at the mess on stage. They just turned away and started talking.

I walked off after one verse. I was terribly humiliated. I failed. I failed karaoke. I failed myself.

Years later, I told Miguel that story. And Miguel is the ultimate showman. I've never seen a room that doesn't light up when that bloke's in it. He'd light up a funeral. He's the happiest human being on earth. When I first met him I wasn't sure if he was putting it on. Could someone be this crazy? Could this man have such energy?

I used to just stand and watch him. He's a whirlwind. It was difficult for me to understand him at first. To learn a language, you need to listen and you'll pick up on those odd idiosyncrasies that are just as much a part of the language as the words. If you start to connect, you'll understand what they're going to say before they say it anyway. With Miguel, and without realising it, he was teaching me. Teaching me to let go, to fly, I guess.

Now, all of us on *The Living Room*, me, Miguel, Amanda and Chris are really tight. Great friends. We have dinners together and we celebrate the kids' christenings, their birthdays, our birthdays, all as one family. And Miguel, who knew about my karaoke failure but also knew about my desire to perform, decided we were going to have a karaoke dinner at his house. Hired a machine. Made the invites. Bought all the food. Revved everyone up about the night. Did everything.

First, there was a barbecue. Miguel cooked with Leonie and Amanda while Sascha, Miguel's wife, prepared the dining table with Kendal, Chris' girlfriend. We all had a bit of fun at Chris' expense because he'd baked homemade bread that was like concrete. We had a few drinks. And then Miguel grabbed the microphone and announced that his dear old friend, me, had a dream to sing karaoke. And tonight was the night. He didn't put any pressure on me, though. He said to me, 'We're all going to sing tonight, Baz. You and I are going to sing together.'

And I was scared. Scared shitless. Leonie pulled me aside and said, 'Miguel set it all up for you, babe. This is all for you.'

Miguel is a beautiful man. Everyone got up and sang. No one does 'La Bamba' like Miguel. Chris has a real edge too. Him and Amanda, you can tell they secretly love karaoke. Even Leonie, who'd never done karaoke or even expressed an interest in it, got up and sang.

And then Miguel gently pushed me to the machine. 'Baz, what song is it going to be?'

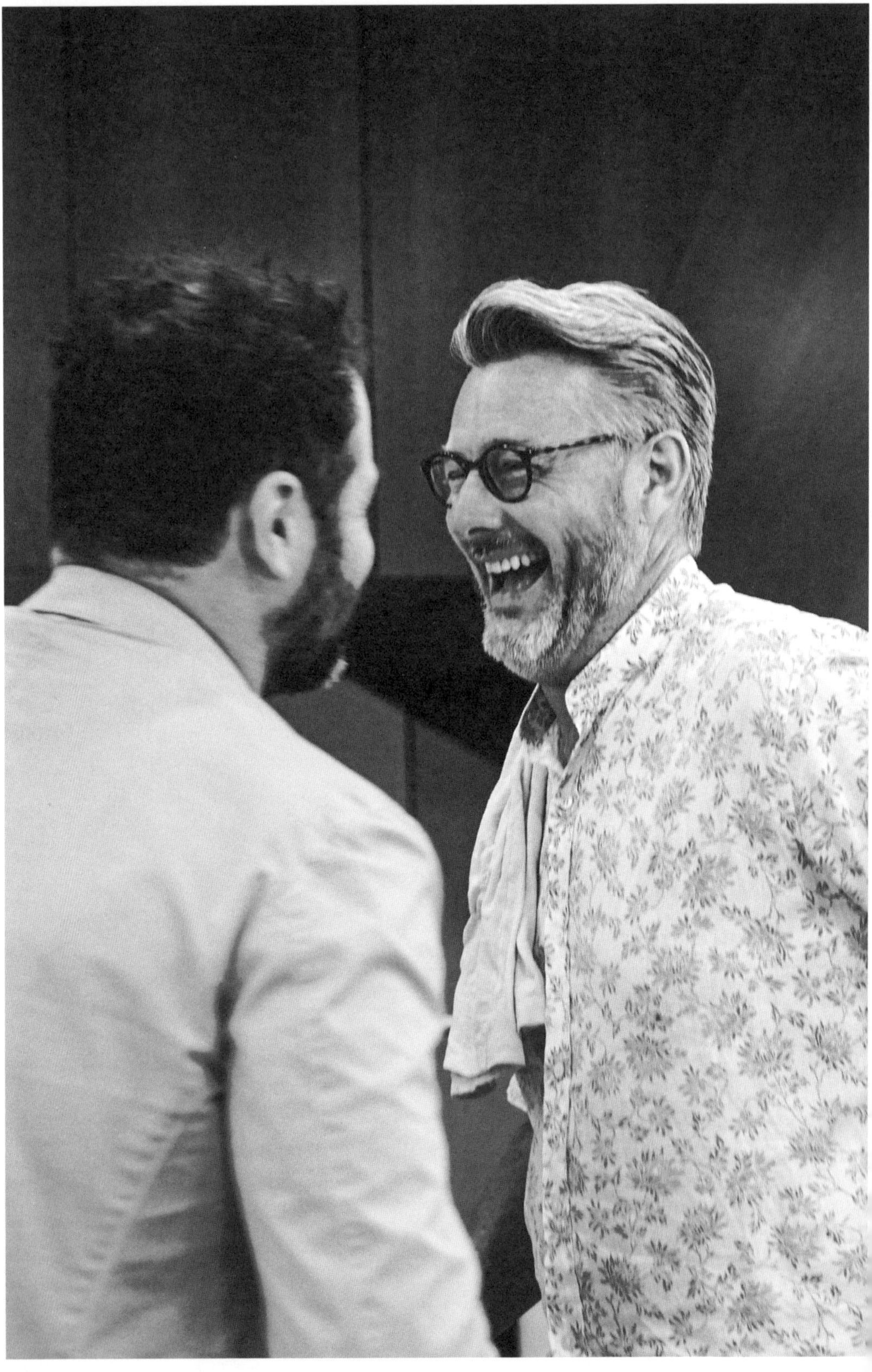

I took another swing at Rodriguez. The words came up. This time in English. As a dyslexic person, trying to read those short snaps of words is confusing. I can't win, right? Amanda's son, Jack, saw that I was crashing and got up beside me and sang. What a beautiful thing for a young boy to sense and then act upon. We got through 'I Wonder' and then I sang the Alan Jackson song 'Drive for Daddy'. My voice wasn't exactly how I dreamed it would be, but I did it. I'd cracked that stupid, irrational fear in the jaw.

That night typified who Miguel is to me and what it means to be a friend. Anyone can prop up a bar and tell you he loves you. Actions shape and demonstrate a man's character, not platitudes. The beauty of what Miguel did was he knew that if he set up karaoke with my closest friends, in his home, in a family setting, and if he prodded me just a little, I might actually do it. He'd gone to incredible lengths to make me feel comfortable.

What did I learn about my karaoke experience? That fun is just fun. People don't judge someone if they're having a good time. I'd never danced in my life before Miguel set up the karaoke even though I'd always wanted to be a great dancer. Now I enjoy dancing. I remember Miguel whispering to me at the Logies, 'Look at us, Baz, a chef and a builder and we're at the Logies. We've got to live every second of this night.' He brings me an energy that I didn't have.

I love the enjoyment I get out of being a dick on the dance floor. I love the enjoyment I get out of not freezing on the karaoke stage now. There's no such thing as failure, really. That's what I've realised. It's just another great day on this planet.

My work with R U OK tells us that allowing people to express themselves in conversation is amazing therapy. The expression of your emotions through song is also amazing therapy. It's what we've done for hundreds of thousands of years. It's in our DNA. You should be screaming. That's how language started, with people screaming from village to village.

I encourage my children to sing. Music is indescribably powerful yet sublime. One of my few regrets in life is that I haven't got more involved in music because I love to express myself.

It's why I'm a storyteller.

The romantic in me wishes I could express myself in love songs.

13
MY SECOND CANCER

For the first couple of years after a cancer, you get checked every two months: blood, urine, protein levels. If it's going to come back you want to get it in the guts and mop up whatever's left.

After we hit the tumour in my neck, and everything started to look good, I got slack. Two months turned into six months, eight months, between checks. I let my fitness slip and got back into long days, and nights, at work. I wasn't meditating. My diet wasn't as good as it should've been and my weight started to balloon.

Emotionally, I was fatigued. There are advantages to having kids later in life – you're not so concerned about money and career, you have more patience and so on, but as you get older you have these underlying thoughts, or at least I do. What sort of world are we setting up for our children with Trump in America, all the school shootings, the Lindt Cafe siege? It all started to wear on me.

Work had been tough. I'm a perfectionist and I felt we could be doing better. I was getting frustrated with life. And then I started to get bad pains in my ribs. When you've been told you've had cancer once, you get a pain and you think, 'Oh, shit, not now … not now.'

It was another layer to my worries. I went in for tests and, typically, you do 'em and go back in two weeks to be told everything is clear. My doctor decided to send me for an X-ray of my ribcage to make sure there was nothing minute in there.

June is full-on in the TV biz. It's a busy, busy time. I was going away on June 24, a month on the boat in Turkey with Leonie and the kids, and I didn't even think to make an appointment to go back. If there was anything, my doctor would call.

Then, while on a shoot at Bunnings, my doctor did call.

'Barry, I need to talk to you. You haven't come to see me.'

'Sorry, mate, real busy.'

'We need to see you. We've got a few problems.'

We agreed that I'd come in two days later, his first free appointment.

More worry. What knocks me around more than anything is the pain I can see Leonie going through. You can tell me anything and I'll be okay. But when I see Leonie is hurt it disturbs me. I feel like I'm letting her down again.

I went to see my doctor. He wasn't joking when he said there were problems: I had big tumours, or multiple myelomas as they say in the game, in both my thighs, my pelvis and hips as well as my lower spine. He told me they were 'structurally large tumours' and that there was a danger that something could break and it could start all sorts of potentially fatal infections.

I had twenty large and lots of tiny tumours creating dangerous levels of protein in my blood. I was hitting ten percent. One percent is acceptable.

The visit and the diagnosis knocked me around. I said to my mum when she was sick, 'As soon as you're better, I'm going to take you on a holiday and we're going to have a great time together.' That opportunity never came because when you're dying you don't come good.

What if this was the start of the end?

I needed to have grace time with my children. If the cancers were as bad as the doctor said, five weeks away wasn't going to make any difference. I needed that holiday and if it meant working even harder on my health and on my mental state when I got back, I was prepared to do that.

I absolutely loved my job on TV and thought this cancer could be the end of my career. I see distance in this career of mine. I was too scared to tell my network executive what had happened. I told my immediate family and I sat down individually with Miguel, Amanda and Chris. They told me, 'Whatever you need, whatever your family needs, we'll do it together.'

That support gave me a certain sense of strength. I remember clearly the show that we recorded on June 24. I had arranged everything down to the final second. I'd finish taping at six-thirty and be on the nine p.m. Emirates flight to Dubai and then on to Istanbul and finally Marmaris where the boat was. The four of us on the show knew what was going on, but no one else in the studio did, so when I left the studio there was a sense of worry, and love, for me from Amanda, Chris and Miguel. I could feel it.

I had an Uber pick-up outside the studio. Leonie was meeting me at the airport with all the bags and the kids. It was weird to walk out of the studio and have people say, 'Oh Baz, great to see you! Can I have my photo with you?', one after the other, and think: no one really knows me. I'm in the worst state of mind I could possibly be in.

The traffic was insane. Even when we got to the airport, it took us fifteen minutes to drive the final five hundred metres. It was like the world was ganging up on me to not let me make the flight.

I got out of the Uber and stood in front of the airport where I knew Leonie and the kids would soon be. Then it came over me. All these thoughts. What if this is the last time? What if this is my last holiday?

And I just ... exploded.

I couldn't control myself. I wept and wept. Tears were pouring out. The what-if thoughts were very painful. It was like a wave of wretchedness.

I cleaned myself up before my family got there. You think you can't let your kids see you cry, but my kids have seen me cry since then and all that happens is

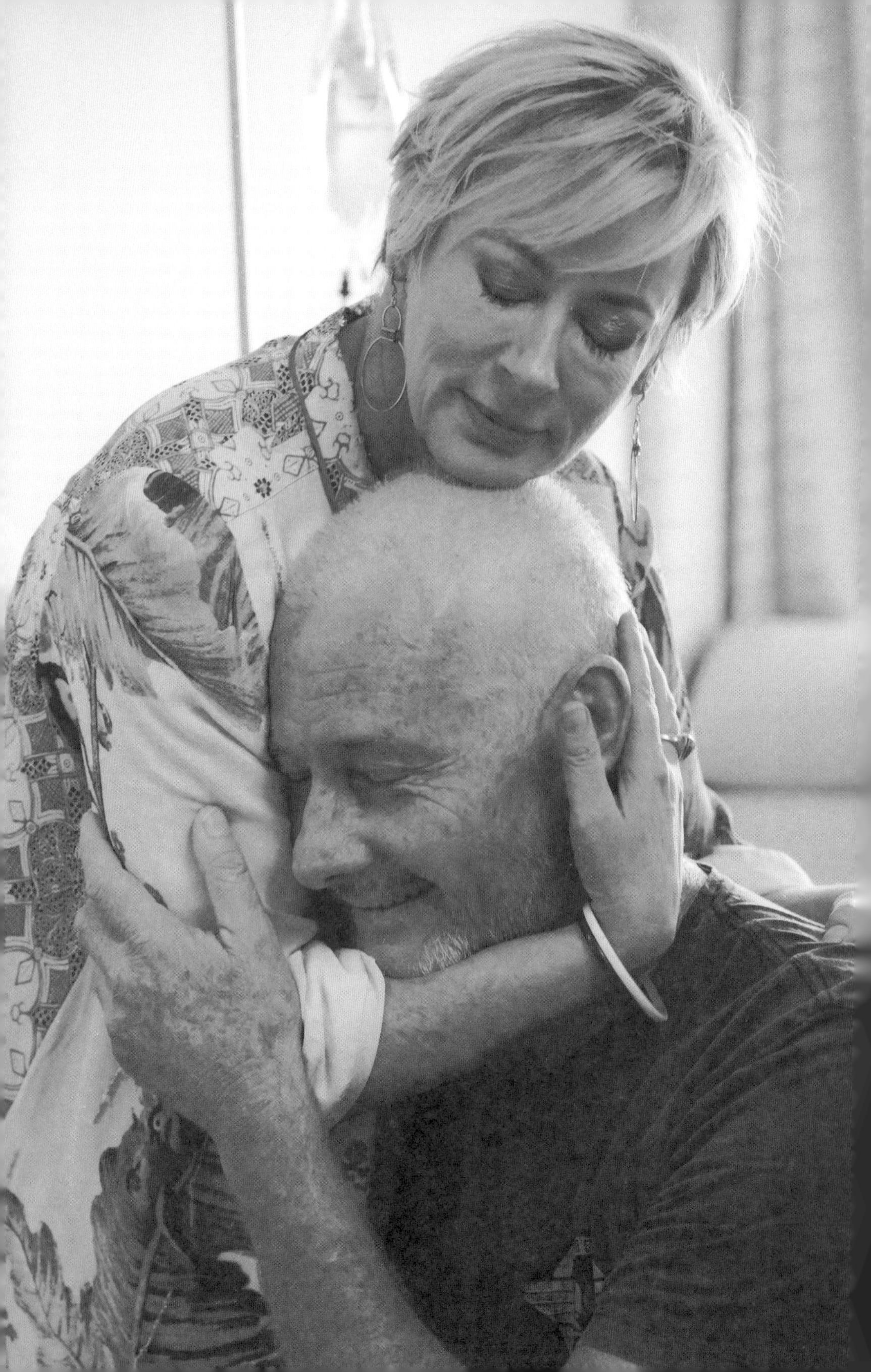

they give me a hug and say, 'You'll be okay, Dad,' just like I'd say to them.

We got onto the plane. I got settled and, all of a sudden, started to feel violently ill. My stomach cramped up. As soon as the seatbelt light went off, I raced to the toilet and started throwing up. Then came the diarrhoea.

When I came out of the toilet, Leonie could see that I'd been unwell. She made sure I was alright. She washed my face. She kept the kids distracted with movies and headphones. The flight attendant asked if I wanted any food. I said no and started wailing again as she walked away. I lay there and I couldn't stop thinking about the return of my cancer. I lost it for a while. I had too much to hold onto. I wasn't ready to let go.

The journey was thirty-eight hours and I was sick for most of it. It was a tough, tough journey. By the time we got to the boat I was exhausted … spent … but a relief came over me. The boat was spic and span, there was fruit on the table, fresh food in its stores and cold drinks waiting for us. The kids were dressed as pirates and crawled over the boat from bow to stern. I got the tender, sparked it up and gave the kids a tour of the marina. We ate at our favourite restaurant. We had ice-creams and the kids swam in the pool.

Before we set sail the following afternoon, I visited a hamam, a Turkish bath. I'd corresponded with other doctors and cancer clinics and they'd said that infrared heat promotes oxygen and blood flow, which is good for tumours. I had a one-hour sauna and started crying. Then I had a one-hour massage and started crying on the massage table. It must've been confusing to the Czech masseuse. I felt like all my emotions were being purged. I'm not saying that infra-red saunas or massage are a cure-all but it worked, mentally, for me. I felt like my anxiety had been nuked.

After a couple of weeks, I had to leave the boat, and Leonie and the kids, for three days of studio. Seventy-six hours of travel for two days of shooting. But I was feeling better emotionally and mentally. I was far more stable. I could do it. The two weeks after I got back on the boat was the icing on the cake, just loving and enjoying my family twenty-four hours a day.

When I got back to Australia, I spoke to one of the executives and we decided we'd share it with the rest of the management. I was worried. I thought it could be the end. First, a replacement host while I was sick followed by a boot into the pasture of forgotten TV personalities.

What do you know? They were more concerned about my wellbeing than any ratings or possible interruptions to the show.

I didn't want to have to explain my story every five minutes. Believe it or not, telling someone you've got cancer is draining. I summed it up like this: when someone asks, 'How are you going? I hear you've got cancer,' you can tell whether they think you'll make it or not. Some people hug you and say you're the strongest man they know; others are more, like, 'Ah well, sorry …' It's like they've given up on you.

The power of the mind is incredible. If you come across three people in a row who give you the look that you're not going to make it, you start to lose faith.

So we decided that we'd share my diagnoses with the people who watched the show. We thought if we could take them with us on my journey, it might give others inspiration.

And there it was.

We cut the crew down to the essentials. We removed the studio audience. How would we play it? We didn't know what to do so we were just ourselves. We ad-libbed. I told my story; Amanda, Chris and Miguel reacted. What came out of it was empowering to me. It was the first time most of the cameramen had heard the story. There were lots of tears.

But there was also belief. The amount of times I heard, 'You'll do it, Baz.' It was like when my dad told me I was the best at everything. If everyone tells you you can do it, you probably can.

If the people surrounding you have doubts, it's tough.

It was two weeks before the show went to air. In the interim, I had agreed to be the MC of a fundraiser for the Many Faces of Cancer, a gig I'd signed up for at the beginning of the year. It was the story of how I had beaten cancer. It was the biggest mind-fuck of my life.

I was in the second round of four cycles of chemo. I had taped an episode of *The Living Room* that announced my cancer was back and was going to air in a couple of days. And there I was carrying this dreadful secret, pretending everything was okay. I was in a room full of people who wanted to get a kiss and take a photo. I tried to not breathe anyone's germs because of my vulnerability to sickness. Even Leonie couldn't kiss me at the time.

Other cancer victims explained to me how my positivity did so much for them.

Like I said, that was a difficult night to get my head around.

The night the show went to air was incredible. I dropped an Instagram post and it went ballistic. Thousands of people were right behind me one hundred percent. I walked down the street and people yelled out things like, 'Yeah, Bazza! Go Bazza!' and 'We love ya, Baz.'

The spirit that can give a man!

I live in the power of the mind.

As it is, once you have cancer, you start getting emails and messages from people telling you they have a cure for cancer. They've invested a hundred grand in alkaline water. Sip of kerosene every day. Only eat apples or wheatgrass or white vinegar or take high doses of vitamin C or cannabis oil. Every snake oil and charm has been shared with me.

The truth is, it's never just one thing that helps you fight cancer. It's not just great gut health or mediation or medicine, it's … everything. It's a Good Whole Life that protects you from mutating cells.

I love what I do. I love that I get to impart a little bit of my knowledge to five hundred or six hundred thousand people every week. People come up to me and tell me I've changed their life. That before *The Living Room* they never would've put grout on a tile or used a handsaw. They tell me I have a way that makes them confident to try.

When you're given a gift like that and you can help charities because of your so-called 'celebrity' status, it's something you don't want to lose in a hurry.

This cancer threatens to take it away from me.

I never think it will, but you have to think it … might …

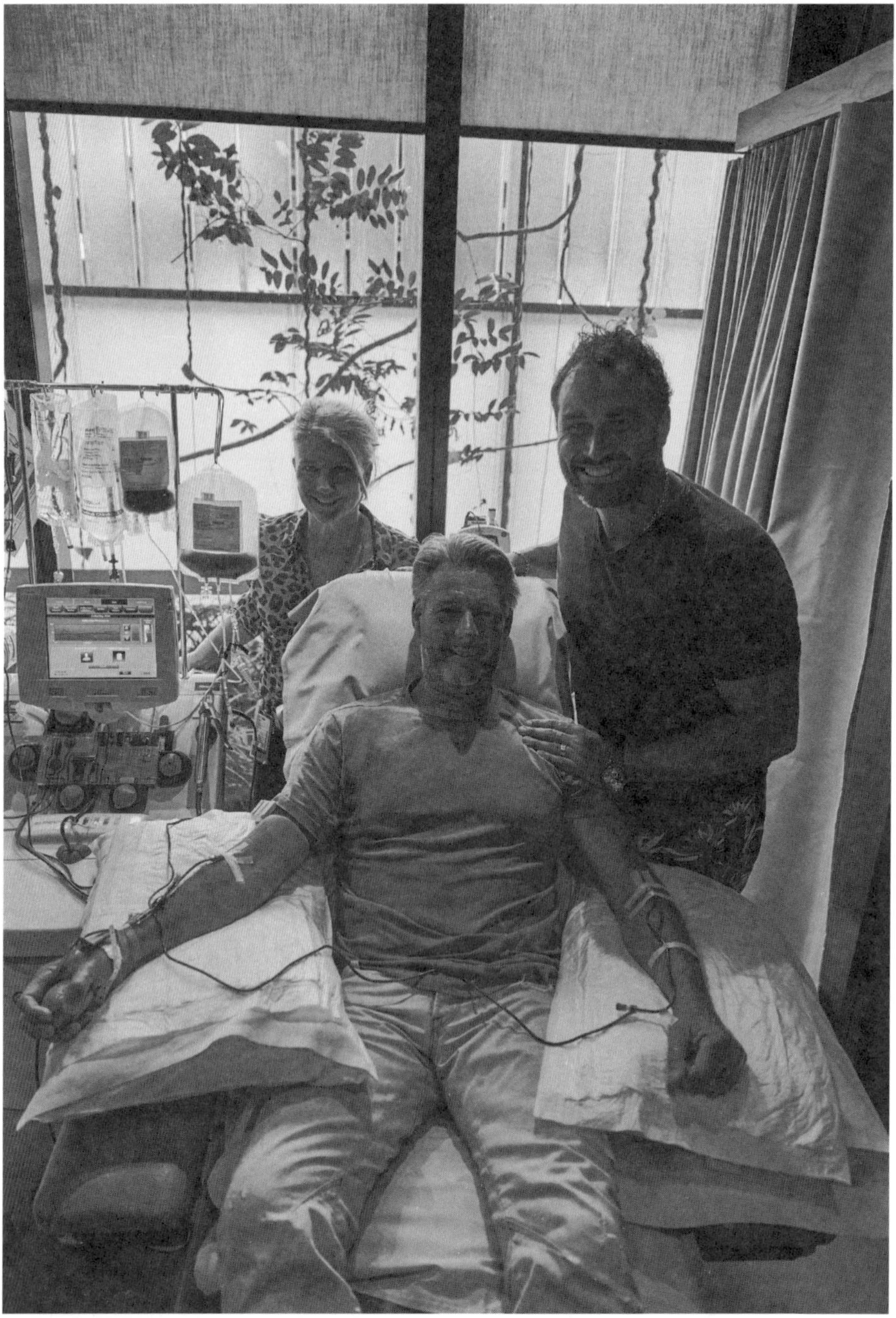

14
SPINNING BLOOD

It's two weeks before Christmas. Thirty degrees outside. The streets around the Kinghorn Cancer Centre in Darlinghurst buzz with drinkers and shoppers. Drivers ride their horns as they fight for prized parking spots on Darlo Road. A conga-line of ambulance traffic pours into the nearby St Vincent's hospital.

Illness and death have no time for an armistice, even at Christmas.

Inside the dramatic one-hundred-million-dollar Kinghorn building (a little aside, all these cancer joints are spectacular architecturally), with its soaring atrium marked by the eight-storey china-and-clay art installation *White Water Falls* by the British artist Richard Long, in the twenty or so lounge chairs, are patients in varying stages of cancer treatment, chemo mostly.

Hardly anyone is doing it alone. A daughter, a son, a husband, a lover, a wife sit in little chairs alongside the patients, some reading, some quietly chatting, but, importantly, all offering their support. It's a lonely feeling sitting in a chemo chair, hooked up. Helps to have a friend to shift the gloom, even if just a little.

The beautiful Miguel Maestre, the Crazy Bull, is my partner today. He's come

LIFE FORCE

from his own visit to a doctor, although for Miguel it's a series of vaccinations for an upcoming family holiday to South Africa. He hates needles. And he has to get jabbed for typhoid, diphtheria and, in Miguel's case 'cause he can't remember the last time he had one, tetanus.

'Ohhhhh, man,' he tells me, 'I couldn't help myself. I looked at the needle going in. And look at you, Barry. You're getting eighteen litres pouring through those pipes.'

A volunteer pushes a trolley filled with orange juices in those little plastic cups with the vacuum-sealed lids that guarantee a Pollock abstract on everyone's shirt and what turn out to be pretty good sandwiches in plastic Tetra Paks.

I'm chair nineteen.

Got here at 7.45 a.m. and I'll be here until three, maybe four. Both arms are plugged via four tubes into an Apheresis machine, a centrifugation device that takes blood out of my body and spins it until the various components are separated. There's a lot of reasons why you might be hooked to the Apheresis, which is taken from the Ancient Greek 'to snatch, to take by force'. It could be a therapeutic plasma exchange, part of an organ transplant procedure, haematological diseases.

I'm here for stem cell collection. Ten million or so baby stem cells to put aside for the main event, a double-hit of chemo, in a month.

The plastic bags hanging from the machine are a rainbow of colours: a bright yellow for plasma, deep red for the oxygenated red blood cells that give us our energy, our strength, clear for the white blood cells that are our immunity and pink for the precious stem cells that'll be taken away in an esky and frozen in sub-zero tanks similar to the ones Miguel and I saw at Chris O'Brien Lifehouse Comprehensive Cancer Hospital. (Chris O'Brien, now there's a man. A great surgeon who, while dying of an aggressive brain tumour, helped to create a one-stop shop for cancer treatment: onco-surgery, chemotherapy, radiation therapy, clinical trials, research, education, complementary therapies and psychosocial support. The whole thing.)

Sitting in a plump upholstered chair for seven hours, effectively immobile because of the four lines in me, gives a man time to think. Takes me back to the feeling of withdrawals I'd get when I'd return from a stint on my boat in the Mediterranean. The feeling of wellness. The joy of being alone with my family on a boat for twenty-four hours a day. You don't take your eyes off your children. Leonie prepares food bought from a Turkish market. The tomatoes are a different colour, the lettuce tastes sweeter. There's love in the air. Smiles. We live in the moment. Sometimes it feels as if we only survive in our city lives for the mortgage. That's why no one stops to talk to ya. Australia has one of the highest cancer rates in the world. Always top three. Turkey? It barely rates. Everyone smokes like a chimney. But where are the takeaway boxes? Where are the packaged foods? Buy from a market. Prepare it yourself. It's a lesson.

I had a decent dose of chemo last weekend. And what chemo does is it kills the cancer in your body and takes a lot of the good cells, too. Doesn't mess around. It's brutal. Feels like it just kills ... everything. Harsh. Horrible. It doesn't have any boundaries. The doctors gave me eighteen litres of fluid over twenty-four hours to flush out the chemicals. If you don't, other organs of your body are more effected.

But, still, I felt dehydrated. Bad headaches. Nausea. The doctor gave me anti-nausea drugs but I figure, if your body wants to expel something, I'd rather expel it. What I was throwing up was vile. It wasn't food. A real acidy taste. Better out than in, as they say. Booze or chemo.

Every afternoon for the past week, I've been giving myself two injections. Straight into the gut. I'm not a needle guy, hate 'em, but it's interesting to note how fast you get used to it. Because I'd always hated needles I wanted the kids to watch me plonk the needle in. Take away the mystery.

Bennett watched first.

'Is it hurting, Daddy, is it hurting?' he asked.

'No, my little prince. It's medicine and it will help Daddy ... '

'It's not hurting? Can I do it too?'

Typical kid.

Those injections make your marrow overflow with stem cells. Lots of pain. It's like there's not enough room in your skeleton. A throbbing pain in my bones, in my lower back, my neck, my shoulders, my ribs and spine. It's like the worst hangover of your life. To take the edge off the pain, I'd go for a walk. When that stopped working, I'd take a hot bath. Then I'd play with the kids. Meditate. Whatever worked, however temporarily.

At night, I'd lie on my bed with my legs elevated against the bedhead. After the chemo, I was getting these ulcerated pimples on my calf muscles. Aches. Even though the doctor scoffed at me ('Whatever works for you, Barry,' he said), it seemed pretty simple to me: because of gravity, all the heavy metals in the drugs had settled in my legs. A week of legs against the wall and the pimples, the aching calves were history.

I tell the wellness physiologist here, Kimberly, about it when she stops to talk.

'Lymph drainage,' she says.

One month from now, after I've had time to recuperate from the chemo, I'll go back into hospital for what they call a 'double fatal' chemo dose. And on the sixth day of treatment, they'll introduce the strongest, most vibrant, pinkest … prettiest … stem cells into my body.

And that will give me life.

15
THE NIGHT BEFORE CHRISTMAS

It's five-thirty p.m. on Christmas Eve. I'm sitting on the lounge lost in a merry-go-round of jolly TV specials. The pine tree glows with lights. A treasure trove of what are probably too many gifts are stacked beneath, awaiting Benny and Arabella's excited little hands.

It's been two weeks since my last treatment for the year, the collection of those pretty pink stem cells, and three weeks since the heavy dose of chemo. The same chemo where sixteen litres of fluid was pumped through me to get the poison out and doctors who told me, 'Sorry, Baz, this time you're going to lose your hair.'

They tell me that every time. I was here seven years ago and it didn't happen. Ain't gonna happen this time either. My rug might've turned silver a little before its time but it's not going to depart its mooring now. Not now.

Anyway, I always tell 'em, 'Losing my hair is the least of my problems.'

In a theoretical sense it is. But here I am, sitting on the couch and my head is itchy as all hell. It has pins and needles, as if hair is sticking into me. It reminds me of the first cancer. The surgeon had to drill holes in my skull to attach a halo to keep my head still for the operation. And those holes, well, afterwards there's a weird numbness you get. Surfers will appreciate this analogy. When you surf in winter your feet go numb but put 'em under a hot shower and they come back to life. They sparkle again. That's the feeling in my head. Numbness and sparks.

I have a little scratch and a hunk of hair comes out. I run my hand through my hair and out comes another hunk.

Now, this is all happening on the couch. The kids are lying on the floor in front of me. What do I do with all this hair? You can't toss it on the lounge-room floor. I don't want to scare the kids. I don't want to stuff the Dyson.

When your hair comes out in your hands you can't help but be struck with the awareness of how real the situation is. It's no longer, this might happen or that might happen. It is happening. And it's an odd feeling because I don't feel sick at all. If I'm going to be honest, I've never felt better. But the chemo is in me. It's smashing the cells in my hair follicles.

Since I can't throw the hair on the floor, I get up and find a garbage bin in the kitchen. It's a strange thing, a really strange thing, to secretly put a part of your body in a garbage bin.

I walk into the bathroom and lock the door.

I run my hands through my hair. A bowl is quickly filled. I flush it away. Another bowl. Another flush. By the fourth bowl I'm wondering, 'Am I going to walk out of this bathroom … bald?' I have an image of Donald Trump. He must wake up to his marbled sink awash with sickly orange strands every day.

The plan before this happened was to get a trendy short haircut and no one would notice, particularly the kids. Is it too late now? I get a lump in my throat. I never really believed that this was ever going to happen. To me? How are my kids going to react?

I can't imagine what it must be like for a woman to go through it. For me it feels as if part of my armour has gone, my strength. The Samson and Delilah story suddenly feels very real, a bag filled with poisonous drugs – my Delilah.

Straightaway, I feel weaker. Even as I walk to the bathroom I find myself walking as if I was older and weaker than I've ever been.

'Snap out of it,' I tell myself. 'Stand up straight and power through!' Easier said than done. I can see how these things can snowball and mentally defeat you again and again.

After the first cancer in 2011, I came out of hospital weighing seventy-eight kilos. I hadn't been that light since I was twelve. I was sore and scared. I was a feeble person. And I noticed that people kept bumping into me on the street. They had no regard for me. And I realised that never in my life had I ever been bumped into in the street. Never. I'd walked down the street for fifty years prior to that cancer treatment and a shoulder had never so much as grazed me. I wasn't the big man any more. My physicality had shrunk. I was a pinball machine. I was human.

It's a fascinating experience, at least in hindsight. People will bump into a small person but they're not going to risk the fall-out of dropping a shoulder into a man who is six-two and well over a hundred kilos. And not many people experience both ends of the spectrum because not many people will drop forty kilos over the course of a few months, transforming themselves from a beast into an old, frail man. A reverse metamorphosis. People would tell me to fuck off in the street. No one had ever told me to fuck off. So I know how fast the mental downward spiral can be. The strain can be incredible and a few aphorisms and pep-talks don't always help.

I go outside and meditate.

I don't do much. I shut my eyes and I walk over to a lift in the black space. I push the button and the lift goes down and down and down and all of a sudden I hit another button and it stops. I walk out to wherever I want to be. Suddenly, I'm surfing a reef-break in Fiji. It's 1999. I remember I got a crewcut just before I went. I was terribly overweight at the time, 115 kilos, about twenty of that around the middle. On the first day, I went in hard for a wave, got a great ride and then got caught in a rip right where the reef bends in from the channel. The paddling exhausted me. I needed a drink but right where the boat was anchored, a rip kept me a couple of arms' lengths away from what felt like a very precious bottle of water. I paddled and paddled until I was exhausted. I barely made it to the boat.

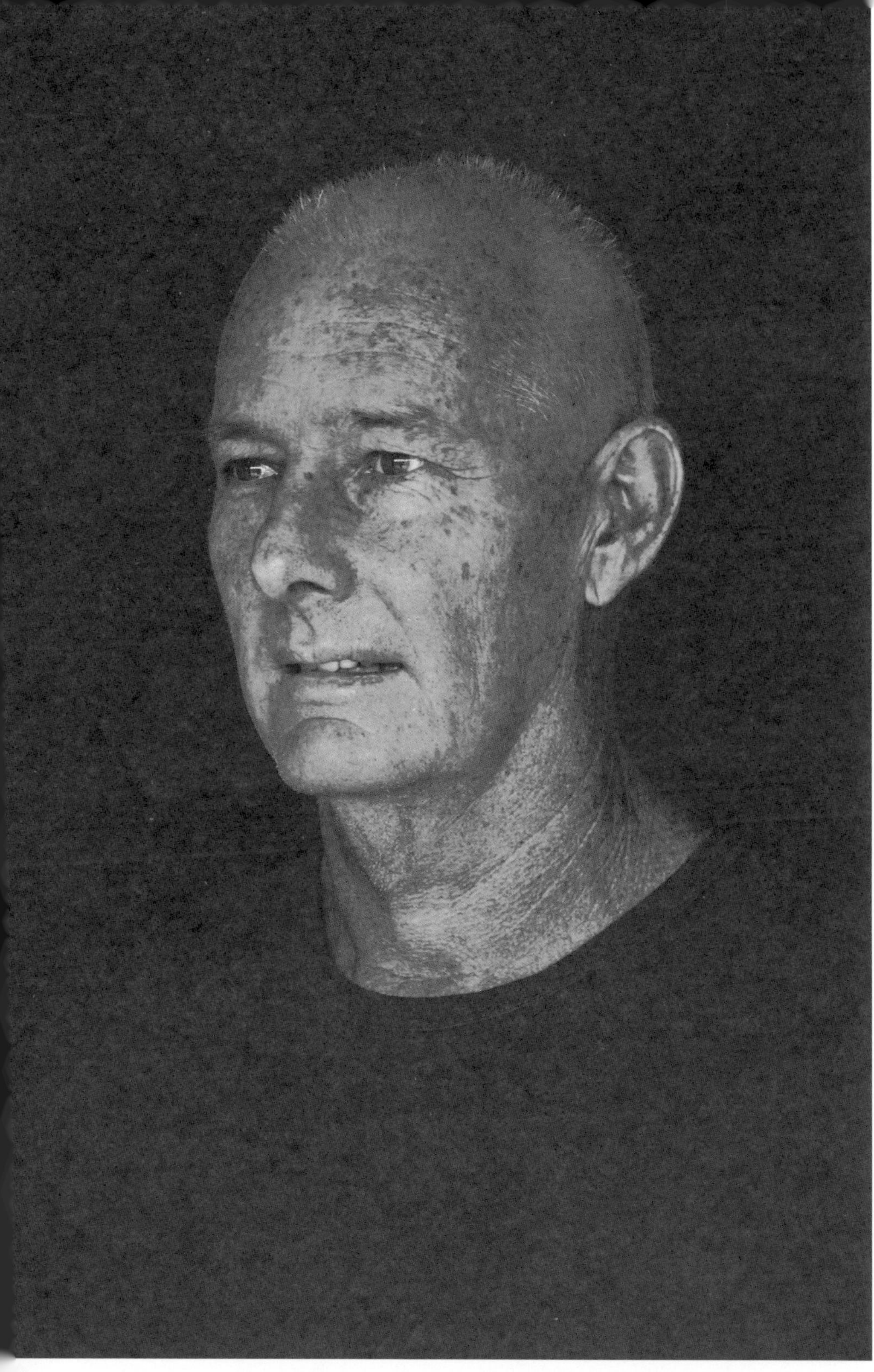

But over the course of a couple of weeks in Fiji, I lost ten kilos and I reckon I put on ten kilos of muscles in my shoulders.

On my last day, I surfed for four hours solid and at the end I hard-paddled back to the boat. This is what I remember in my meditation. Me: strong, wearing a crewcut, feeling as if I could hold the world in my hands and shake it. My meditation switches to a man I met earlier in the year. I was with Amanda Keller doing a TV segment and this guy came up, shook my hand and told me how inspiring it was that I was sharing my cancer journey. He told me he'd gone through exactly the same thing one year earlier and showed me before and after photos. Quite frankly, it looked as if he'd been in a health club not being shot full of poison.

He told me that in fifty percent of cases, your hair grows back differently. He looked in great shape. Better shape than me. Told me how the cancer was a wake-up call. That he'd transformed his life for the better.

I open my eyes. I smile. I let it go.

I'll get a trendy short haircut and see how it flows.

16
THE EFFECT OF MINDFUL MEDITATION

In the previous chapter, I talked about meditating to escape the dark thoughts of my kids seeing me lose my hair, seeing my mortality, on Christmas Eve.

Meditating has helped me – wait, more than helped me, it's lifted me – over those moments when I've felt overwhelmed by stress.

I do it everywhere. In my car. At my desk. On a beach.

If I feel mentally tired, I'll close my eyes and sit with my hands on my knees and take a couple of deep breaths. By the third or fourth breath, I'm feeling this beautiful, clean air entering my body. It gets cooler with each breath and I can feel the freshness coming in through my nostrils. I imagine the air as being so beautiful and so perfect it inflates my lungs into these giant balloons.

After a few moments, I'll open my eyes and look across the room. And it's there that I'll see the lift I described earlier. In my mind, I stand up, walk over to the lift, and at this stage I'm really concentrating on my breath, feeling it hit the hairs in my nose, coming in and going out of my lungs, and I push one of the up-down buttons.

Sometimes it takes a few seconds, but the doors open. I take another breath of beautiful air and step into the lift. Inside is a wall of numbers. I push one at random. I never see what the numbers are but, then, I take a deep breath and as I start to blow I hear this ... ding, ding, ding! ... and the lift takes me down, down, down or up, up, up depending which button I hit. When I'm ready to take another breath it stops.

As I breathe in, the doors open. What happens then is the air that comes into the lift, and into me, is purer and cooler and even more beautiful than before.

I step out, stand there for a second and look at everything around me. Sometimes it's the beach, sometimes it's the jungle, sometimes it's the front of my boat. I'm the only person there. There might be birds in the sky or fish in the water but the air is pure and it's all mine.

I concentrate heavily on the air going in and out of my body. I focus on everything that I can see, the glitter on the water, how the sky meets the ocean, the rocks on the mountains.

When I'm ready to come back, I take a few more breaths and step back into the lift. As I breathe out, the doors open and I walk over to an imaginary desk where I sit down.

I take two more deep breaths and open my eyes.

And that's my little trip away. I've done that for fifteen years. When I was depressed and I couldn't take it any more, that's where I'd go.

When cancer hit me the second time, I began to study mindful meditation. It's the next level. It's not about imagining pretty beaches or a serene mountain. It's about being in the present moment and nothing else.

The Buddhists call it *sati*, which means mindfulness. An awareness of things. There's plenty of data that shows it has a powerful effect on what they call 'mood disturbances'. In other words, it gets you out of a black hole.

Being mindful takes you to a deeper level. You only use your brain for what's happening in the moment. When I'm walking on the beach, I'll be up to my knees in the ocean and I'll acknowledge things are happening, the traffic, whatever noise there is, but then I put it aside for what is actually happening: the hairs on my legs moving in the water, the sand under my feet and how the grains move with each step, the salt water coming into my body, the warmth, or cold, of the water.

Mindful meditation gives your brain a complete rest. It gives it time off from fear and uncertainty and pain.

And still more data shows that this resting of the brain has a curing component. That it can actually impact at a cellular level, that it can energise your immune system.

It ain't no cancer cure. What it is, is an important part of a Whole Life. A complement to medicine and science and nutrition.

Even if you're not sick, who doesn't want to experience, deeply experience, the exquisiteness of each moment?

Want to feel grounded? Want to feel better? Close your eyes. Breathe.

LIFE FORCE

BARRY DU BOIS & MIGUEL MAESTRE

17
THE BIG HIT

It's Wednesday 31 January and I'm about to get pumped full of deadly chemicals.

This is the where my treatment goes nuclear. Doctors don't like to call it a 'Double Lethal Dose' of chemotherapy, but if you do a little searching online that's what it is. I've never believed in beating around the bush so it seems a little pointless to sugarcoat things now.

Doctors say the treatment, if that's what you can call it, buys most people an extra five years of life. When they die it's not because of the illness they had, in my case the multiple myelomas or blood cancers, but the ferocity of the chemicals. The chemo's job is to wipe out as many cells as it can and in the process it's going to reduce my immune system to nothing.

No one talks about curing the cancer; this isn't a cure.

I'm six-two (186 centimetres if you like it that way) and ninety-eight kilos, strong as a bull, fit as a trout etc., and my doctors says I'm looking at ten to fifteen extra years. Which, at this point in the game, I'll take.

I think about that day in June 2017, when I took a call from a private number.

It was the doctor who is treating me now, and who treated me for my first cancer. He asked me why I hadn't come in to see him after my last test and I said, 'Well, if there was something you would've called.' And he told me there were substantial problems. My elevated protein levels meant there were big tumours somewhere.

'Things have changed, Baz,' he said.

I told him this couldn't possibly be happening now. I was about to take Leonie and the kids on a five-week trip around the Med on the yacht. I said I desperately needed the holiday, that it had been a hard year, and what happens if I stay, something goes wrong and we miss out on our last holiday together?

We agreed I'd go on holiday and when I came back I'd do the three-cycle chemo – which would turn out to be four cycles – do a stem-cell retrieval and nuke the tumours with the double dose chemo shortly after Christmas.

I was scared to tell work. I thought I'd lose my job. Fortunately, they were incredible to me and said they'd do whatever they could to help. I told Amanda, Chris and Miguel at the same time as Leonie and they all rallied behind me and gave me some needed strength.

The five weeks with the kids and Leonie cruising the Med, living in each other's pockets twenty-four hours a day, eating the freshest food, was a love-fest. I came back to Australia fitter and happier than I'd ever been.

I'd been having second thoughts about the treatment. Who wouldn't? There's no doubt about it, the cancer is going to kill me, but how soon? I have a philosophy. If you're going to put a seed in the ground, you've gotta water it. You don't just toss it and walk away.

In for a penny, in for a pound, you could say.

Once committed to The Big Hit, I do everything to prepare for it. I get my diet right so my gut is ready. I exercise: surfing, paddling, walking along the beach. I meditate. My protein levels, which indicate how aggressive the cancers are, are at zero. In one sense, I'm a picture of fucking health. If they shot me I'd live. If a truck hit me it would bounce off.

I know I can beat this. I have to put muscle on because the chemo is going to affect the muscles. I'll just keep working harder and harder, eat better, and do everything I can.

There's a guy who's the same age as me down the corridor and they don't think he's going to make it. The whole family is in there crying. Do I feel lucky? In one way, yes. In another way, and what I want to get through in this book is that there's more to this whole cancer battle, journey, whatever you want to call it, than putting yourself in the hands of doctors and waiting for what they say is the inevitable. Mum, dear Mum, rode that conveyer belt straight to her death.

You can help yourself. You can improve your situation.

All the things I've been doing have helped me immensely. Doctors don't like to talk about alternative therapies but, for me, and as complementary therapies alongside my cancer treatment (rather than an alternative to it) – as plenty of data is starting to show – some can work and they really can help.

I'm admitted into St Vincent's Private at eleven a.m. Which is a weird sorta time. It's not the start of the day or the end. It's like those mid-afternoon flights when you've checked out of the hotel but you've still got a whole morning to fill. So I did all those menial things you do to kill time: take the garbage out, get the pool filter right, shuffle paper on my desk.

I get wheeled into the operating theatre. My arm is straightened and, under a local anaesthetic, an incision is made below my clavicle and a central line is inserted into the big vein that goes to the heart.

Straight up, I'm pumped full of fluids.

The idea is to saturate your organs. What is going into you is deadly. In building terms, before you wash bricks with acid you hose 'em with water and then you spray the acid. That way, the acid only sticks to the outside with the muck and the mould and the debris. If the acid were to get inside the brick, it would weaken it long term. Doctors want my organs as moist as they can be.

I fall into a depression on my first night in hospital. It isn't hard to get upset in this sickly place, this horrible little room with the forgettable print on the wall.

It's a long night full of dark thoughts. Depression or fear? I'm not sure.

The statistics show that if I do get the ten or fifteen years the doctor predicts, and remember the clock is already starting to tick, I'm very lucky. That makes me seventy years old when I die.

I must … just … make my kids' twenty-first birthdays.

For a man like me who thinks he's going to be around forever, when those two worlds collide, when reality punches you in the face, it creates fear.

And on a practical side, have I done enough to prepare myself for what's going to happen in the morning? The nurse gives me an anti-nausea pill but it actually calms me down. Eventually, I get a couple of hours of sleep.

The following day, I get hit with 200 mg of Melphalan, the chemo drug, for each square metre I am. Which means, for a bloke like me who's two square metres, I get 400 mg, or nearly half a litre. It takes an hour to pump it into me.

The nurse tells me to prepare for the worst and says that soon I'm going to be in agony.

'You're in for it,' she says.

According to her, I won't be able to open my eyes, I'll be spewing every five minutes and I'll be lucky to make the dash to the dunny most of the time.

I wait.

It doesn't come.

I feel great.

Wait, I don't feel … great … but I'm not in agony. My eyes are open and I've sucked the hell out of endless ice cubes to stop the chemo causing ulcers in my mouth. It ain't a lot of fun when you have sensitive little snowflake teeth like me but I push through it.

My doctor swings by to see how I'm doing. He's surprised I haven't been knocked around. I tell him my hair seems locked in for the ride, too.

'Oh, it'll go. It'll go,' he says with a sympathetic smile.

Is this as bad as it's going to get? A cramp here and there? A bit of mild diarrhoea? I feel pumped, really pumped. All that good nutrition has paid off. He even tells me the kids can visit so long as they don't have a cold or feel poorly.

I go down to the gym at the Kinghorn Centre next door and knock off five minutes on the stationary bike. I'm not going to win the Tour de France but the endorphins I get from the exercise make me feel the happiest man alive.

It's funny how life goes. I'm a strong-headed guy but yesterday I was defeated. Today I feel like I could run around the block with my kids strapped to my back.

Let's face it, I've had a lethal dose of chemo and even that can't kill me! Fuck, that's a good feeling.

Maybe I won't get as sick as people are saying.

'Am I the strongest bloke alive?' I joke to the nurse.

She smiles. It's a pained smile.

She knows what's coming.

And it does.

Two rough nights in a row.

All the promised effects of chemotherapy rain down on me. The vomiting, the diarrhoea, the loss of appetite, the beautifully named mucositis (an inflammation of the mucous membrane in the digestive system), the pain.

I'm in bed, breathless. Going to the bathroom is hard. I can't drink.

It feels like the worst hangover of my life.

And, let me tell you, I've had a few …

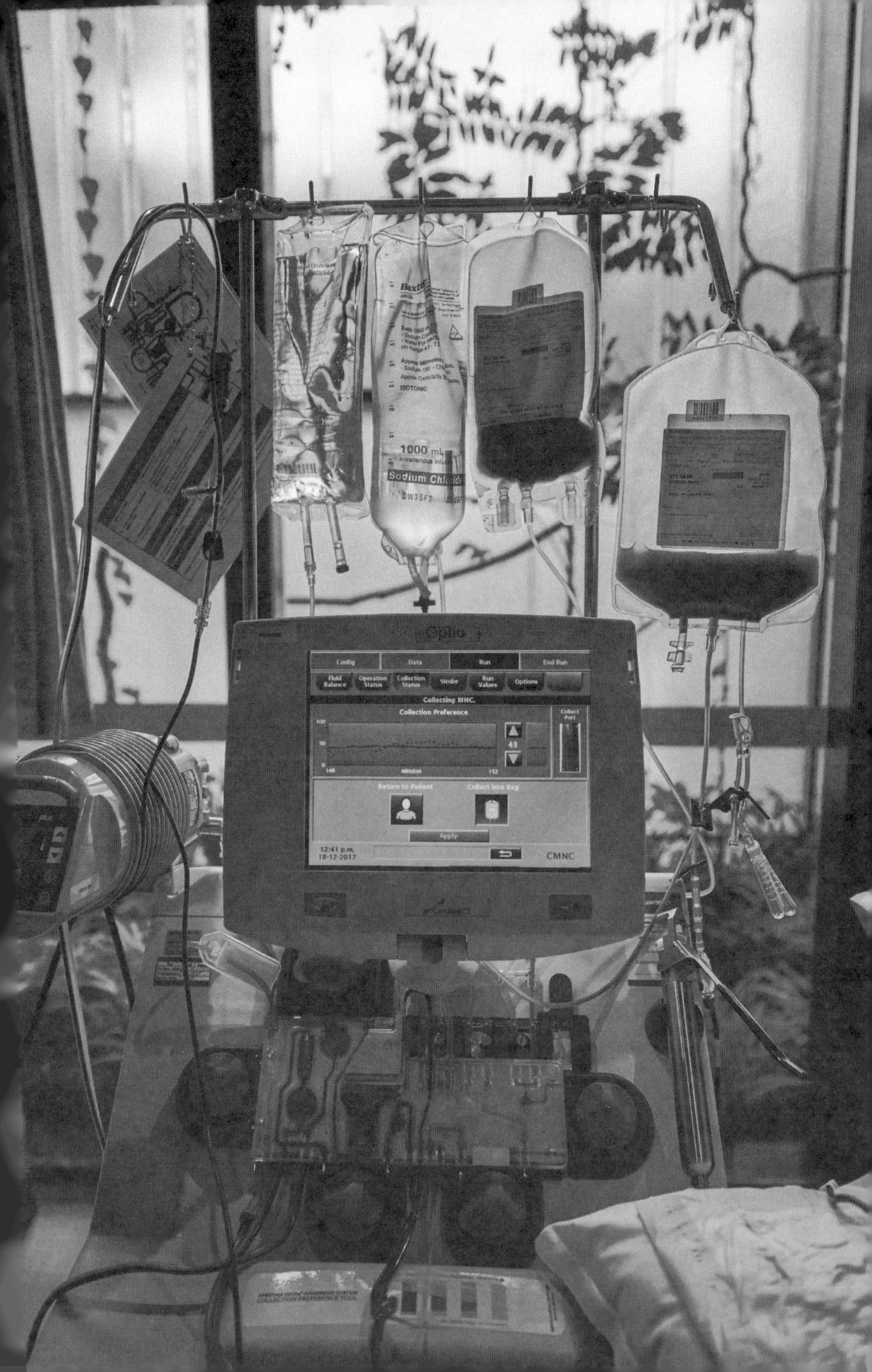
1000 mL
Sodium Chloride
ISOTONIC
Config
Data
Run
End Run
Fluid Balance
Operation Status
Collection Status
Strobe
Run Values
Options
Collecting MNC.
Collection Preference
43
minutes
Return to Patient
Collect into Bag
Apply
12:41 p.m.
18-12-2017
CMNC

LIFE FORCE

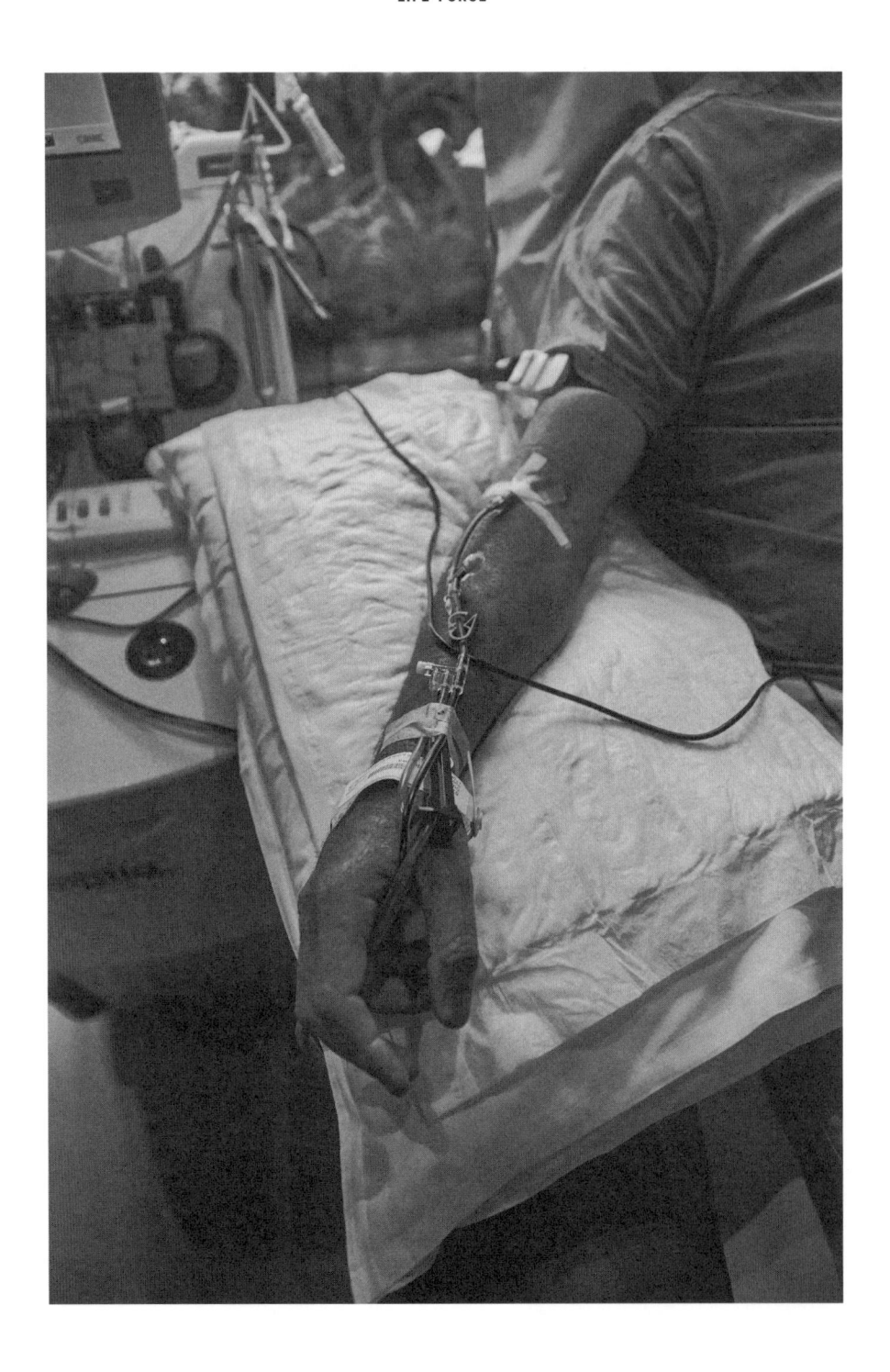

18
HUMANITY

I almost died last night. Of the dumbest thing. A bit of tinea between my toes had caused an infection that could've hit me in the heart. My fever was off the charts. My foot was swollen and hot. My leg felt like it was burning. Angry red tracks zig-zagged from my foot to my calf. The doctor told me he'd seen big men like me knocked off within four hours from infections like this.

When you're having a double hit of chemo you have zero white blood cells. You have no protection from infection. You're on your own.

I thought I was gone. As the poison moved through me, I felt weaker and weaker. My temperature kept rising as the drip containing the antibiotic was hurriedly set up. My leg and foot started to boil. I was surprised how quickly it could go bad. When I asked the doctor if I could have a quick shower to wash off the cream Leonie had put on me when she'd massaged my legs and back earlier in the day, he told me the antibiotics couldn't wait. They had to go in now. Five minutes could've been the difference between life and death.

I gotta say, twelve days into the double hit and it has been … rough. All that talk in the previous chapter about being superman and avoiding the worst and then a little spew at the end, thinking that was rough? It's serious now.

The thing about a big hit of chemo, in my case with four hundred milligrams of it in me, is you can't hide from it no matter how immortal you might think you are.

You feel really, really sick.

I don't want to be crude, or cruder than I have to be, but if you want honesty, this is it. Personally, I don't believe in using blocking drugs for diarrhoea. If it needs to come out, it should come out. I also believe if you can keep the fluids up, you don't need anti-nausea drugs either.

But what happens when you spew constantly is you lose the lining of your stomach and even more of your ability to fight the disease. From the vomiting, your throat all the way to your gut becomes ulcerated. Even if you want to eat, which you won't, you're breaking up infected blisters with each chew and swallow. That has waste product in it and it ends up in your stomach so there's even more acid down there.

It feels like the worst curry joke ever. It's like having a six-inch piece of old broomstick stuck in your arse and every time you sit on it, it pushes further into you.

The thing with my first cancer, and Leonie's cancer, was they were specifically located cancers. It was a point-and-shoot job for radiotherapy. No sickness. No diarrhoea.

With Mum it was straight into chemo. She never had much information. There were no complementary therapies. We tried Chinese medicine, liver cleansing diets, meditation, we sent her to retreats but there was no real interaction with doctors about combining all these methods.

I remember being in the waiting room in Wollongong and there were thirty patients in there. I was in a queue of death. The people were just numbers, waiting for their drugs and then they'd go home and die. The front ones would drop off and new ones would join at the back. It was like a bad sci-fi movie. That was when I took her to Sydney only to be told it was too late.

When I came in for The Big Hit I was scared. All they've got left to fight my cancer is this big dumb weapon called chemotherapy.

Like they put into my mum.

After five days here, I thought I'd come through the worst of it. I gave myself a little pat on the back.

But the nurses knew.

'You'll get sick,' they assured me. 'Everybody gets sick.'

I thought I was different. I was going to get through the tough part and be spared the worst because I'd eaten so well, I'd had plenty of sleep, I'd exercised and I'd meditated. I was in the best hospital in the country, my family was all around me and everything was just … working. As my good friend Lorna Jane says, you've gotta have good nutrition and movement. Move. Nourish. Believe.

The doctor had said, you might get through the chemo but you've gotta watch the infections. He said most people get an infection from a bug in their bowel or skin. From all the testing, we knew there were two types of bugs in my gut. Every five days when we do a swab from the back of my throat, the back of my nose and test my stools and urine, we know there are two. But they hadn't multiplied.

Then came … tinea.

Let me backtrack to the day I came in here. It's not like a car or bike race where you're in the pits, you check the car, you fuel it up and ten minutes before it starts you put your gloves on and the starter says, ten, nine, eight …

You sit there in a leather recliner with the curtains drawn on the summer sun and you think, 'What's going to happen next?'

By not being aware, you become very scared.

In my case, a nurse came in with a smile as wide and lit up as a Christmas tree. She could've been an angel.

She told me she was going to take me down to the theatre where the doctor would insert the central line into the vein going to my heart. Normally, when you're having chemo they put it in a vein in your hand or your arm. But the veins there can only take so much. The sort of chemical that's going in me, and the volume of it, can collapse those veins.

So the nurse took me down for the procedure.

Humanity is a funny thing. I believe in Maslow's Hierarchy of Needs, a theory of psychological health by the American Abraham Maslow. It's usually presented as a pyramid. At the foundation, we need air, food, water, sex, homeostasis and excretion. Then, safety, employment, family, health, property, followed by love and belonging, esteem and, finally, self-actualisation.

I hadn't felt much of that humanity, that warmth, that belonging, in the hospital. Then she grabbed me by the hand, squeezed it, smiled at me and said, 'You're in a great space here. These guys are the best of the best. They'll look after you.'

At that stage, it could've been butchers with knives and I wouldn't have cared. She gave me security and safety and belonging.

Treatment isn't just medicine. And it's not just complementary therapies. It's a combination of everything.

A quick tip. If you're going through chemo, never … think of farting. It'll be the biggest mistake you've ever made.

Sorry.

Anyway, after they'd administered the antibiotics for the infection, I started to get sad and a bit teary-deary. It was a hot night and my temperature going up wasn't making life easier.

Then the nurse said, 'It's hard being positive all the time. So how about I make your bed for you?'

She put a new sheet on the bed, tidied up the room, changed the blue blanket for a white blanket, folded it back, got two plastic bags filled with ice and put 'em in pillow slips. Then she put the pillow slips into the bed and told me to put 'em under my arms to cool me down.

It's amazing how when you're at your worst the touch and attention of another human can bring you through. It's why the Whole Life approach is so important.

I woke up in the morning full of life again. The doctor came in and told me my white cells were back up. Everything was up. The antibiotics that I'm often so negative about and refuse to use unless the situation is desperate, saved me.

The nurse who got me through the night helped me to my feet and we had a cup of ginger tea with a slice of lemon and some honey.

Happy days.

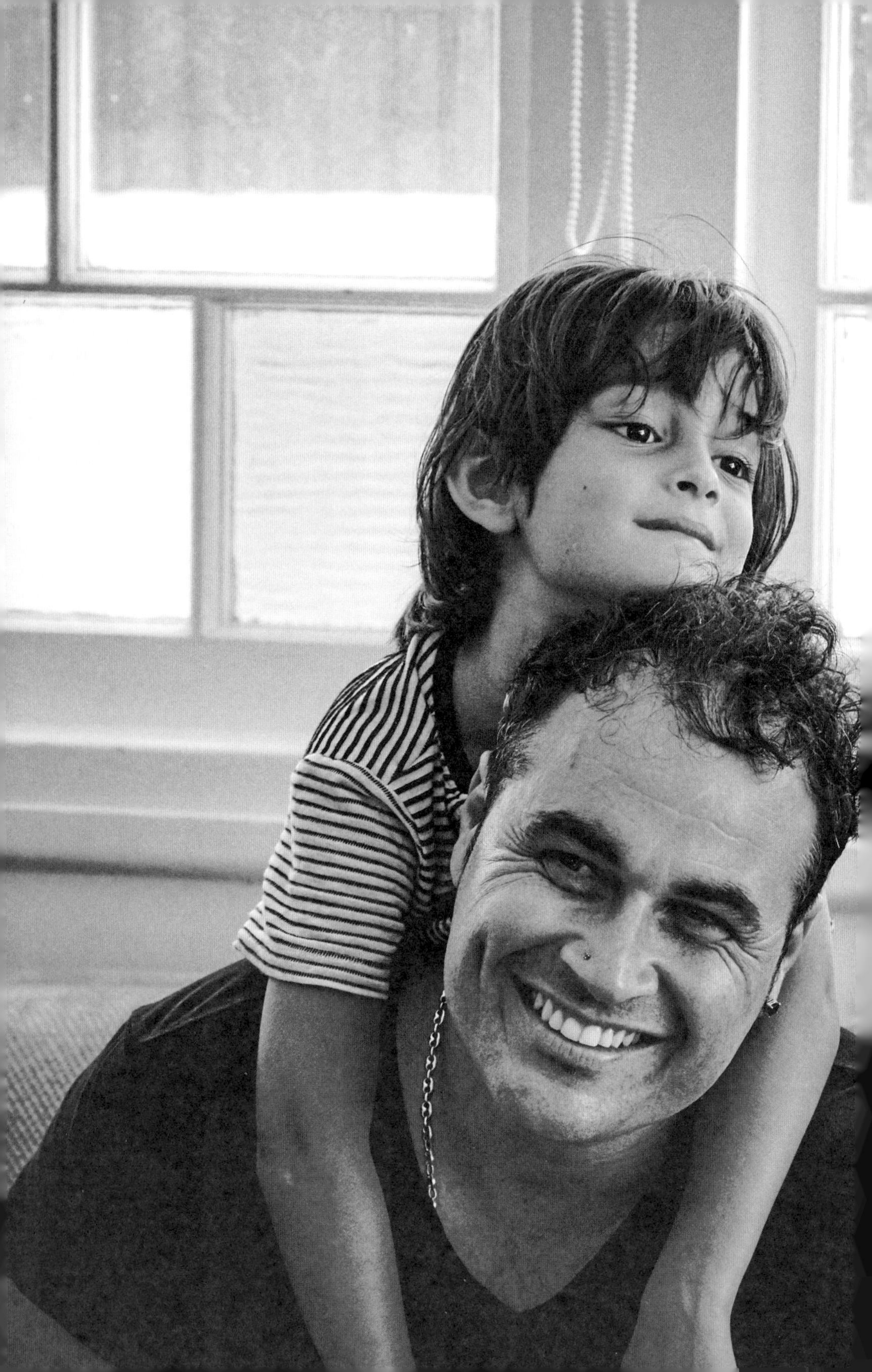

PART TWO

LIFE FORCE

NOURISH YOUR BODY AND SOUL
BY MIGUEL MAESTRE

I love Barry. I love Barry. I love Barry. I loooooooooove Barry! Is that too much?

I remember seeing him for the first time when I auditioned for *The Living Room* seven years ago. Barry walked on to the auction set with his long hair swept like a wave off his handsome face, with his designer clothes, and he was already famous from *The Renovators* by this point, and I thought, 'This guy is minted!'

We clicked from the first moment. Barry is very warm and he makes everybody feel comfortable in whatever room he's in. He's the kind of guy who will throw a Christmas party and invite the CEO of Channel Ten as well as the runner who brings the coffee. Barry bought his big house in Bondi because he wanted to have space to bring people in. More than that, he wanted a welcoming home for his children to grow up in.

I talk with Barry all the time about his cancer. I make myself do it, even when it makes me sad or gives me dark thoughts afterwards. I had an experience with a friend of mine, Stephane, who had lung cancer. We'd worked together at Bathers Pavilion, a fancy restaurant at Balmoral in Sydney. He was a hard-ass French guy who set up his pastry section next to me in the kitchen and he used to give me shit, say my fish was no good, my sauce was no good.

It was crash, crash, crash, crash. Amazingly, we became very good friends. I even became the godfather of his son, Hugo.

When Stephane got sick I avoided talking about it. He was very young, not yet forty-five, and he was a very strong person. Cancer and death wasn't something we talked about. By not talking, I missed out on hearing how he felt. Just before he passed away, he was still looking quite good. We had lunch together and he said, 'Miguel, all I want is for you to look after my boy when I die.'

I said, 'Fuck, Stephane! Don't talk shit like that! You're not going to die!'

I was the one who kept brushing it away. He was trying to talk about the things that mattered, about a reality that was negative. I don't know if it was the devil's fault or if it was my fault, but I wasn't there when Stephane died. I didn't think it was going to be his last weekend. I was working, I was busy, and he'd texted me and told me he was fine.

The guilt of not being there has followed me since then. That was four years ago and it's still there in the shadows. That's why he asked me to promise to look after his son. I should've gone and seen him that weekend. I should've been with him all the way to the end.

I have to live with that.

I like to keep Barry busy. Recently, he was in hospital and he posted on Instagram: 'I'm so bored!'

I said, 'Barry, why don't you get the family to come in?'

'I don't want anyone to come and see me.'

'Barry, what the fuck? We're your family and your friends. We can come and see you. We're going to share with you! What are you thinking right now?'

'I'm thinking not very nice things.'

That's what I mean. If I was there, we could be looking at stupid things on Instagram: people falling over, beautiful architecture. We could be sharing. Barry told me, 'Miguel, I don't want anyone to see me like this.'

Barry is a strong man who doesn't want to see his weakness. It affects me. When I drive I think about it a lot. I feel confusion, I'm scared and I'm really worried. Sometimes I call him and he's not well and I can hear it in his voice. He tells me about those dark moments when he can't sleep at night because of the steroids. Everybody else in the house is happy and relaxed and he's there, alone in the dark, contemplating his mortality.

But instead of pushing it to the side, I do everything I can to be with Barry. I always think about how I can be with him more. I call him all the time.

'Barry! I need help with my backyard deck! Barry, I need a fence! Barry, can you help design a pool for me!'

We talk about the need to externalise your feelings. We work with R U OK together and it has taught us the importance of being open about your feelings. I'm a Spanish man and usually the head chef. We're not meant to say 'I'm depressed' and shit like that.

We need to destroy the taboo. Everybody is affected by cancer in some way. I was just in the local pharmacy and the lady there was going through the cancer process and she shared it with me because she'd seen *The Living Room* episode where Barry told the audience his cancer had returned. There was no awkward silence. You need to think of cancer like the flu, a very bad flu admittedly, but let people say, 'I feel like shit, I feel scared.'

I've got this massive water bomb of stress in my mind. Whenever I talk about Barry's cancer with someone, a few drops leak out and it relieves the pressure.

My fear of Barry's illness gets me very stressed and keeps me on edge. What can I do? I know if I put a lamb shank in the oven for six hours it's going to be fucking delicious.

Food!

It's what I can do, it's all I can do.

This chapter takes you through food you can prepare before, during and after your or your loved one's treatment.

I had great meetings with Dr Judith Lacey, the Head of Supportive Care and Integrative Oncology at Chris O'Brien Lifehouse Comprehensive Cancer Hospital. I learned the specifics of cancer and the treatments and how the patient needs to be strong before they go through it all, and how that can be achieved through pointed nutritional combinations.

I know how to make a churros that will blow your mind. Just add four hundred grams of sugar! That isn't going to work here.

These recipes will keep you nice and juicy! Nice and tight! We want you to be hydrated, to eat calorie-dense foods to minimise weight loss and to supercharge your immune system for the fight of its life. During the recovery process you'll be buggered. It'll feel like you've gone fifteen rounds in a boxing gym. We've created foods to make your energy levels soar.

What a pleasure it was to write and create these recipes. All of them are easy and quick to prepare. I want to encourage friends and family to make and bring these foods into the wards. It brings a fresh energy into a room that might be filled with negative energies: sickness, worry, anxiety.

Walk in with containers of delicious foods and the first thing everyone will talk about is how good it looks and smells. The conversation will move away from sickness and into, 'How long it did it take to cook? How did you cook it?'

Food is a gift. The greatest thing in life is sitting at a table with your family and friends enjoying a big home-cooked feast.

Arriving at the hospital with flowers and sitting there saying, 'We're all really sorry' and 'This is terrible' doesn't make you feel like there's a happy ending coming.

Here, we have little snacks to eat, to keep you going during the day, to keep your weight and your spirits up.

Barry and I want to inspire people to think about their lifestyle and what they're doing with food.

To think about how they treat their children, to be aware that sticking them in front of TVs and screens and giving them takeaway junk isn't the right thing to do. Everything we do affects the final result.

A lot of the food here is designed to just make you feel better about yourself. I'm not an expert. I'm not a doctor. My qualifications are basic; it's a pot and a pan. Together with a dietitian, we've created some really nourishing food, and it tastes so good you wouldn't think it could possibly be good for you.

I know Barry's story won't be a sad ending. It's going to be a very happy ending. The happiest.

BARRY DU BOIS & MIGUEL MAESTRE

A HOLISTIC APPROACH
BY DR JUDITH LACEY

When caring for the whole person, getting to know a person and what helps them thrive is so very important.

When Baz and I first met in my clinic at Chris O'Brien Lifehouse Comprehensive Cancer Hospitalt, it was pretty intense. Baz was still dealing with the new diagnosis of his disease returning, and was worried, as most people would be, about the impact it could have on his life and the life of his family and friends. The two of us had to get to know each other, and work out what he needed to help him through his cancer journey.

I was immediately struck by how beautiful a person this guy was – a heart of gold, authentic – and how open and vulnerable he allowed himself to be. I quickly learned of his love for his partner and two children, his 'other family' from *The Living Room* whom he adores, that he's an R U OK ambassador and all the many other wonderful things he does. So it was pretty clear that this guy needed to be present, to have energy, to keep giving and somehow find ways to nurture and be nurtured. He needed to be able to keep functioning during his upcoming chemotherapy and have a good strategy to help him through his stem cell transplant. And he needed to share his experience with all those out there who love him, and to work with his gorgeous friend, Miguel, to create this book.

When faced with a diagnosis of cancer, it is often hard to know what to do next and how to move forward. But a cancer diagnosis can be the experience you make it and one that, with time and good support, can become a journey of growth and resilience.

I always start by asking people what their main concerns are and how they think I can help. My role as a doctor working as a specialist in supportive care and integrative oncology is to provide a holistic approach to helping people live well with their cancer, irrespective of the stage of their illness. It is all about personalising an approach to care and being flexible as needs change throughout the cancer journey; empowering people to be involved in their own care; and using an integrated approach: combining Western, evidence-based complementary therapies and exercise to improve and maintain wellbeing – physical, psychosocial and spiritual.

Cancer is not one disease but a collection of different diseases, and while there are some symptoms and side-effects that many people with cancer share, such as fatigue, anxiety, pain and sleep disturbances, each person's experience is different. Personalising our approach to treating the cancer and the effect on the person is the way of the future. Baz wanted to be proactive in trying to minimise the effects of his treatment on his day-to-day life and be in the best possible state for recovery. This is where exercise, diet, mind-body therapies and other complementary therapies can make a big difference.

So Baz and I talked a lot about coping and stress management strategies, symptom management, physical fitness, being mindful of listening to his body, the safe use of herbs and supplements and, most importantly to Baz, nurturing and supporting his body with good diet and the right foods.

I love the idea of nurturing and healing through food. So much is written about food and cancer. In so many cultures and traditions, food is central to family and social interactions, and central to nurturing and healing. With traditional medicines like ayurvedic medicine, Chinese medicine and modern natural therapies, the focus is on what we eat, our gut and the role it may play in our physical and mental wellbeing. One of the greatest challenges with cancer is the impact of cancer therapies on our ability to eat and enjoy food, and managing nausea, altered taste, appetite loss and weight changes. Some great questions Baz and I explored were: How does what we eat impact on our wellbeing, immune system and our daily energy level? Can what we eat influence our health? What about the many so-called anticancer diets out there? The role of probiotics and the gut microbiome? Sugar? Meat? Preservatives? Antioxidant-rich fruits and cruciferous vegetables? Where do herbs and supplements fit in? Which ones are safe, which could be helpful?

Regaining control of one's life is a theme that commonly comes up for people with cancer. We are always exploring, with our patients and their families, ways to stay in control, maintain dignity, cope with uncertainty and empower the pursuit

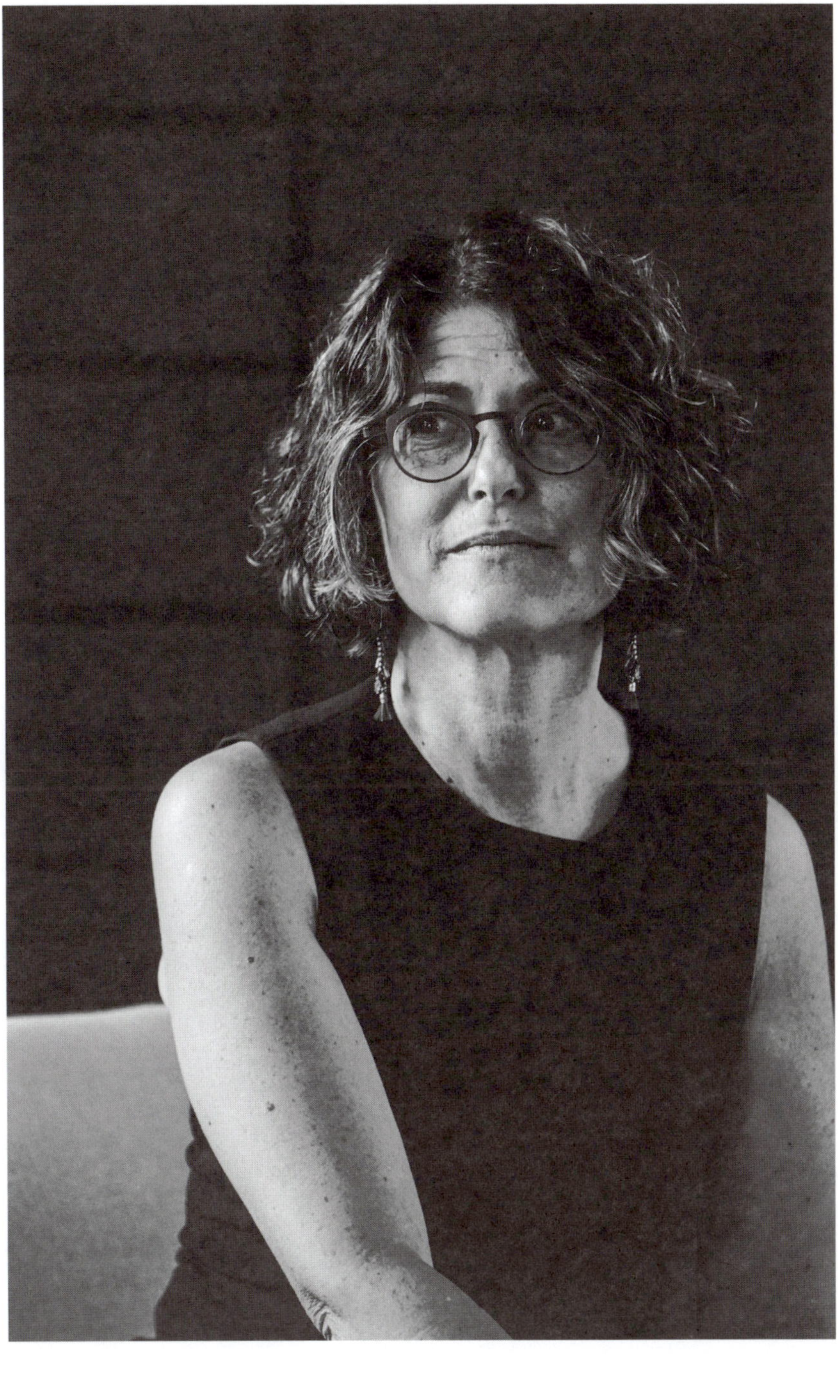

of wellness. Food can be a way for family, carers and patients to stay in control, to nurture and be nurtured and to maintain wellbeing. For some people, there is great benefit in seeing a psychologist or counsellor, and there is also great benefit in working with the mind-body connection through mind-body therapies.

Introducing Baz to mindful meditation was easy; this was something he was seeking and embraced. Mindfulness is a well-recognised practice in cancer care, for patient as well as practitioner. It enables one to face any situation in a calm, present and engaged manner. Baz and I discussed the different mind-body therapies offered at our centre: yoga, Qigong and mindfulness. It was mindful meditation that worked so well for Baz when dealing with the road ahead and the side-effects of his treatment.

Exercise is now a huge part of cancer care, and can be a very important part of building a resilient self. A session with the exercise physiologist produced a personalised exercise program for Baz to work with at home. It is one of the most useful therapies we can prescribe for cancer-related fatigue and some other symptoms. Baz was so taken with the exercise program that he had ambitious plans to set up an exercise bike in his room during the stem cell transplant. Typical Baz!

It is negotiating the right fit for each person that makes my job so fulfilling, in addition to working with an excellent team that provides this multidisciplinary approach to care. I often refer to it is a having a toolbox full of wonderful tools; the art is choosing the correct tools for the individual and then knowing how to put them to use.

There is nothing more satisfying as a healthcare professional than helping empower and support people to achieve personal wellbeing and improve their daily quality of life. It is such an honour to work side by side with these wonderful people, Baz and Miguel, who have created this book to help people embrace ways to live well along a cancer and life journey.

Judith Lacey
MBBS, FRACGP, FAChPM (RACP)
Head of Supportive Care and Integrative Oncology, Chris O'Brien Lifehouse
Senior Clinical Lecturer, School of Medicine, University of Sydney

BARRY DU BOIS & MIGUEL MAESTRE

THE SIMPLEST JOYS
BY MERRAN FINDLAY AdvAPD

Meeting Baz and Miguel for the first time, it was impossible not to be struck by the warmth of their genuine friendship and their passion for good food and nutrition. They came to the table with an idea, proposed with such engaging enthusiasm that it was easy to be swept along.

'A book that highlights the importance of nutrition for someone living with a cancer diagnosis,' they said. 'You know, like a guide to support people at one of the most challenging times in their lives when nutrition is so important.' Little did they know, they were preaching to the already converted. We immediately embraced the unique opportunity to bring together an impressive team of chef, integrative oncology doctor, oncology specialist dietitian, and of course the ultimate expert – the patient. The team goal: to assist those trying to navigate the confusing world of nutrition information to optimise their cancer care and, ultimately, quality of life. Like many, Baz and Miguel share a passion for good nutrition and quality food, yet perhaps even more importantly, the pleasure of companionship over a meal with loved ones, one the simplest joys life offers.

As an Advanced Accredited Practising Oncology Specialist Dietitian dedicated to the field of cancer nutrition for close to two decades, I've heard people describe the experience of a cancer diagnosis as akin to being on a 'bullet train'. Others have said they felt they were on the 'conveyor belt' of appointments, tests and treatment regimens, all before having a chance to comprehend what was actually happening. When so much feels out of your control, taking care of your individual nutrition needs or those of someone you are caring for, can often feel like the one thing left in your power to influence.

Cancer and its treatment can place extra demands on the body, making nutrition care even more important. Scientific evidence tells us that being well-nourished during cancer care significantly improves outcomes. But what happens when this simplest pleasure becomes a challenge? Treatments such as surgery, radiotherapy, chemotherapy and other anti-cancer agents, can affect your ability to maintain adequate nutrition because of common side effects such as nausea, vomiting, taste changes, reduced appetite, painful swallowing, mouth ulcers, altered digestion and absorption of nutrients, and changes in bowel habits to name just a few. Unintentional weight loss, even if overweight to begin with, can lead to cancer malnutrition, muscle wasting and fatigue. During these times when food intake is reduced or when needing to promote healing and recovery, nutritional strategies can provide positive assistance with meeting your individual nutrition goals – whether this is by increasing energy (calories/kilojoules) and protein or modifying dietary fibre intake according to your side-effects and symptoms.

We tend to think of cancer as a single disease, when in fact it is a grouping of many different diseases. So it follows that understanding the cancer diagnosis, intended treatment and expected side-effects is important to determine your individual nutrition priorities. These can sometimes be quite different to what your body needed before your cancer diagnosis and can shift throughout treatment and recovery. Whether it be in my clinical practice, university teachings or education of health professionals, it's clear that navigating nutrition care is something that consumers and clinicians alike find challenging. Comprehensive nutrition assessment and counselling with an accredited practising dietitian can assist with individual nutrition advice before, during and after treatment.

With a cancer diagnosis comes an overwhelming number of questions and those relating to food, diet, nutrition and lifestyle are common. As is so often the case, there is a bewildering range of information available. Unfortunately, there is an equal amount of misinformation, even from people who can be well-meaning but misguided in their advice. In an era where it seems anyone with a blog is a self-anointed nutrition guru, I encourage those seeking advice regarding cancer nutrition to be a discerning consumer – look for cancer-specific information and advice from reliable sources, produced by credible organisations and supported by the best-available evidence. Seek help and advice from health professionals with appropriate qualifications who specialise in the field, such as an accredited practising dietitian. These skilled professionals form part of the multidisciplinary cancer care team who work together to deliver optimum care. Eating well and good nutrition shouldn't cost a lot of time or money, nor should any practitioner make promises of curing cancer through diet alone. Although I wish this were the case, it simply isn't true. Be wary of unbelievable claims – if it sounds too good to be true, it almost certainly is. Radical or restrictive diets can mean your body gets too much or too little of certain nutrients, which can cause problems. Basically, doing anything in extremes rarely leads to a good outcome so aiming for balance is key – even though something is freely available without requiring a prescription, it doesn't necessarily mean it's either helpful or harmless.

While it seems common sense to suggest that someone who is well-nourished will have better outcomes, a better response to treatment and is more likely to recover quickly, the evidence consistently supports this. We very much hope that this book is the start of the conversation regarding the vital role of nutrition in comprehensive cancer care.

From the outset of creating this book, it became evident that this is a very personal journey for Baz and Miguel, a celebration of life and friendship. Cancer is personal. It affects almost all of us in some way. The joy that nutritious food can bring, whether it is through eating, preparing or cooking, can be the catalyst for moments of normal life and to support each other during cancer care. Through shared meals with loved ones we also honour our culture and traditions. These reasons are fundamental to the inspiration for this project – to our patients, caregivers and families; our dedicated team of health professionals, thank you for the privilege of allowing us to care for you through listening to your needs and to strive to deliver the best care possible.

To Baz and Miguel, I would like to say thank you for creating this incredible opportunity that we are sure will help so many. Thanks to the magic of Miguel 'The Crazy Bull' Maestre's tenacity and creativity in the kitchen, we have compiled a series of recipes, supported by science, categorised to help with meal selection according to how you're feeling that day. Find a friend, a happy, peaceful place to eat and most importantly – enjoy!

Food with friends and family. How life should be lived.

Merran Findlay

MSc (Nutrition & Dietetics), BSc (Nutrition), Grad Cert (Paediatric Nutrition & Dietetics), Advanced Accredited Practising Dietitian

Executive Research Lead-Cancer Nutrition, Oncology Specialist Dietitian – Royal Prince Alfred Hospital, Sydney Local Health District

Oncology Dietetics Clinical Research Fellow, Chris O'Brien Lifehouse Comprehensive Cancer Hospital

Adjunct Senior Lecturer, University of Sydney

LIFE FORCE

A WORD ON FOOD SAFETY

Most people are aware that food safety and good hygiene practices when preparing food are important to reduce the risk of becoming ill from foodborne bacteria. Whenever you're cooking, it is always important to: wash fruit, vegetables and herbs very well; and cook eggs, poultry, seafood and meat thoroughly. However, for those living with cancer and undergoing treatments that suppress the immune system including chemotherapy and stem cell transplants, these practices are even more important due to the body's reduced ability to fight infection. If you are unsure how this advice relates to you, please discuss with your care team.

If you are preparing food for someone with cancer, being familiar with food safety advice, including high-risk foods to avoid as well as safe food handling and storage practices, is essential.

For further information, please refer to the Food Safety advice outlined in the Cancer Council Australia Nutrition and Cancer resource:
www.cancercouncil.com.au/cancer-information/managing-cancer-side-effects/nutrition-and-cancer/food-safety/

Remember to check for any special instructions if you plan to take food to friends or family when you visit as there are extra travel tips for transporting food. For further advice, please refer to health service guidelines in your state or territory such as NSW Health Guidelines for Bringing Occasional Food to Patients at:
www.cclhd.health.nsw.gov.au/ourservices/nutrition/Documents/Guidelines_for_Bringing_Occasional_Food_to_Patients.pdf

---

NOTE: all the following oven temperatures are fan-forced, so adjust according to what you cook with at home.
Eggs and chicken should preferably be free-range and organic.
  Enjoy!

BARRY DU BOIS & MIGUEL MAESTRE

NUTRIENT ANALYSIS

Nourish and Nurture – Making Choices Easier

To help make choices that suit individual nutrition needs, we have highlighted key properties of Miguel's delicious recipes, such as dishes that help increase protein or fibre intake. Knowing which recipes provide softer options and those that are lower in spicy or hot ingredients can also be useful depending on how you're feeling that day.

Higher protein

A cancer diagnosis can often mean individual protein requirements are higher than usual. Extra protein may be necessary to promote healing and recovery, particularly from cancer and its treatments. Choosing options higher in protein can assist with meeting these increased needs and are often nourishing if your appetite is poor or you are experiencing unplanned weight loss. Nutritious and delicious, Miguel brings some of his family favourites to the table.

Softer option

Sometimes cancer treatments mean softer meals are easier to manage. Miguel has included his and Barry's favourite drinks, desserts and soups to nourish and nurture – soft and soothing! It's important to discuss with your care team for individual advice if you find swallowing difficult or painful.

Higher fibre

Some cancer treatments and medications can cause constipation. Including meals that are high in plant-based fibre from fruits, vegetables, nuts, seeds, cereals and grains can help keep bowels regular. It's important to drink enough fluid and keep up with some gentle exercise or activity to help the dietary fibre do its job. Alternately, some people with cancer may find reducing fibre intake temporarily can ease their bowel symptoms. If this is the case, try selecting some of Miguel's delicious recipes without the higher fibre tag. If you have ongoing bowel symptoms, check in with your doctor or dietitian for individual advice.

Lower spice/heat

Cancer treatments can cause symptoms that make your mouth sore or easily irritated. Miguel's Spanish heritage means lots of flavour and he has also given options if you find you need to choose meals that have less spicy or hot ingredients.

Nutrient Analysis of Miguel's recipes was conducted in order to classify each of them into the categores of higher protein and higher fibre using FoodWorks9 Professional Edition (Xyris Software (Australia) Pty Ltd). Data sources for the analysis were the AUSNUT 2013 and Ausfoods 2017 nutrient databases. Nutrient analysis was undertaken by Corinne Cox, Accredited Practising Dietitian.

Calculations were based on quantities as stated in the recipe and generic products where possible. All dairy products used were full fat (i.e. full cream milk and yoghurt). If a size or measurement wasn't stated in the recipe then 'average' or 'medium' size was used in the analysis. Recipe yield was calculated based on the maximum number of suggested serves for each recipe.

Substitutions

Alternate milks (such as soy milk or lactose free milk) and flours can be substituted in most recipes for those with dairy or gluten intolerances or for reasons of personal preference. Although Miguel cannot guarantee the end result will be the same, it should still taste great!

COOKING FOR BAZ

LIFE FORCE

BAZZA'S MOST FAVOURITE TURMERIC LATTE

This is a Barry all-time favourite. Baz is in love with turmeric lattes as he doesn't drink many coffees like I do. He loves them very much every day; when we are filming, you can see how much he enjoys them. I came up with this recipe full of flavour and, for me, the secret is after infusing the milk or almond milk with all the flavours, froth it like the coffee shops to get that effect of a latte. Cow's milk provides higher protein.

Makes 2 Lattes

1 small knob fresh turmeric, peeled (about the size of a thumb)*
1 small knob fresh ginger, peeled (½ size of thumb)
1 tbsp almond butter
1 tsp pure honey
220ml milk or almond milk
1 pinch cinammon
1 cinammon quill
pinch pink flaky salt
¼ tsp pepper (Leoni's touch)

Blend all ingredients except the cinnamon until smooth.

Pour into a medium-sized saucepan, add the cinnamon quill and warm over a medium heat, until nearly boiling. Pour into a mug and serve.

If you have a coffee machine you can use the frother for more a foamier latte effect.

*Turmeric is known to interact with certain chemotherapies and some other medications. Please consult with your doctor for individual advice. Source: Memorial Sloan Kettering Cancer Centre, Aug 2017. About Herbs, Botanicals and Other Products, https://www.mskcc.org/cancer-care/diagnosis-treatment/symptom-management/integrative-medicine/herbs/search

THE LIQUID HULK, BAZZA'S FAVOURITE SMOOTHIE

Baz always wanted a drink that would quench his thirst and, as he is in love with coconut water, I came up with this smoothie that put a smile on his face. Baz has lost a lot of his muscle mass during treatment but, to me, Baz is like the Hulk – very strong. Sometimes real strength is not in muscles, it is in an attitude of wanting to get better, and let me tell you something … my great friend Baz is definitely stronger than the Hulk himself. Cow's milk or soy milk provide higher protein options.

Serves 2

300ml coconut water or milk
⅓ cup frozen mango chunks
⅓ cup frozen pineapple chunks
⅓ cup frozen paw paw chunks
1 banana, sliced
3 big (massive!) handfuls English spinach
1 tsp matcha powder
2 tbsp almond butter

Blend everything together in a high speed blender and serve immediately.

TOMATO GAZPACHO

The best way to refresh your body and pack it with all the good stuff is having gazpacho, the cold Spanish liquid salad that will make you just feel good about yourself. In every Spanish tapas bar or restaurant they will serve it in the hot days sometimes even with ice cubes, the origin is in Andalucia and is every single ingredient of a salad blended to a perfect cocktail of goodness

My favourite part of the gazpacho is that when you order it in Spain the waiter will come with a tray full of chopped ingredients like Manchego, cucumber, jamon, croutons and you finish your own at the table

If you make too much gazpacho and have left over it freezes very well making the most delicious icy poles in the world.

Serves 4

500g ripe oxheart tomatoes
½ red capsicum, deseeded and finely chopped
1 clove garlic
½ cucumber, peeled
50ml olive oil
2 tbsp sherry vinegar
1 slice white bread
salt flakes

TO SERVE
2 hard boiled eggs
croutons, grated
1 grated carrot
½ cucumber grated

Blanch tomatoes by immersing in boiling water for 30 – 60 seconds then cooling immediately with iced water. Peel off the skins. Add all ingredients to a blender, blend until smooth then pass through a fine sieve and chill for 1 hour.

Serve in soup bowls garnished with croutons, grated carrot, cucumber and diced hard boiled egg, with a big splash of olive oil.

This recipe freezes really well into icy pole molds for a refreshing snack (leave out the egg).

SOFTER OPTION • LOW SPICE

LIFE FORCE

PUMPKIN SOUP

When your appetite is gone and your mouth feels sore, there is nothing more heart-warming than the feeling of a delicious velvety pumpkin soup. This recipe is easy and perfect to bring in a thermos when visiting at the hospital … better than flowers!

Serves 10

1.6kg butternut pumpkin (approximately)
sea salt and freshly ground black pepper
½ bulb garlic, roughly chopped
6 rosemary sprigs
½ bunch thyme
½ bunch oregano sprigs
1½ tbsp olive oil
2 onions, peeled and chopped
1 leek, chopped
2-3 whole garlic bulbs
pinch freshly grated nutmeg
30g grated manchego cheese
1L hot chicken stock or veggie stock
70ml double cream
15g butter
roasted baby beets for garnish

SOFTER OPTION • LOW SPICE - *omit pepper*

Cut the pumpkin in half horizontally and remove the seeds. Score the pumpkin flesh using a small sharp knife and season with salt and pepper. Rub the pumpkin flesh with the cut garlic, then lay the rosemary, thyme, oregano sprigs and whole garlic pieces in the centre of each half. Drizzle both pumpkin halves with a little olive oil.

Put the pumpkin halves in large roasting trays and roast for 1–1½ hours, or until tender. (The exact cooking time will vary based on differences in oven temperature and the variety, shape, density and thickness of the pumpkin.) The pumpkin is ready when you can effortlessly slip a knife into the thickest part of the flesh.

Remove from the oven and allow to cool. Once cooled, remove the rosemary and garlic from the pumpkin and reserve the garlic. Scoop out the pumpkin flesh and set aside.

Heat the olive oil in a large saucepan. Add the onion and leek and stir frequently for 5–6 minutes until translucent, but not browned.

Scoop out 2–3 cloves of the reserved roasted garlic and add to the pan along with a touch of seasoning and pinch of grated nutmeg. Continue to sauté for a further 1–2 minutes. Add the pumpkin flesh to the pan along with the grated manchego and stir together.

Pour in the stock, bring to the boil then reduce the heat and simmer for 10–12 minutes. Stir in the double cream and heat for a further minute.

Blend the soup until smooth. Add the butter and blitz again until you get a bright shiny, smooth orange texture. Pour the soup into a clean pan to reheat.

For the garnish use roasted baby beets or other roasted veggies.

MAMMA'S CHICKEN SOUP

One of the things that Baz always told me at the peak of his treatment was that he couldn't eat and a nice chicken soup would always be the easiest thing to put in his mouth, because it is comforting, warm and nourishing. This one is a great feel-good dish. It is served with pasta and fills your tummy and also fills your heart with positive thoughts. If you are going to visit your friend or your family, home cooking is the best – it creates a great positive energy just talking about the food and starts great conversations. My own experience when I catch up with Baz is that he always gets excited talking about food and, to tell you the truth, Baz is not really a foodie but there is something magical about home cooking that makes people happy.

Serves 10

3 tbsp extra virgin olive oil
4 brown onions, diced
2 leeks, diced
1 garlic head cut in half
⅓ bunch thyme, leaves only
4 bay leaves
2L cold water
1 whole chicken, around 2.5kg
½ celery head, chopped into chunky pieces (finely chop the leaves to garnish)
4 carrots chopped into chunky pieces
500g wholegrain macaroni, or similar shaped pasta
salt & pepper
4 eggs for poaching

Heat the olive oil on a medium heat in a large saucepan and sauté the onions, leeks, garlic, thyme and bay leaves for about 6 minutes until soft but before they start to colour. Add the water and chicken and bring to the boil, then simmer for 45 minutes.

Add the celery and carrots and cook for a further 5 minutes, then remove the chicken, pick off the meat, cover and keep warm.

Add the pasta and follow cooking directions on the packet, but 3 minutes before it's ready, season with salt and pepper and crack the eggs into the broth, Poach for 3 minutes until the pasta is al dente.

To serve, place some chicken in a bowl, add an egg then ladle over stock and vegetables, and garnish with celery leaves.

HIGHER PROTEIN • SOFTER OPTION • LOW SPICE - omit pepper

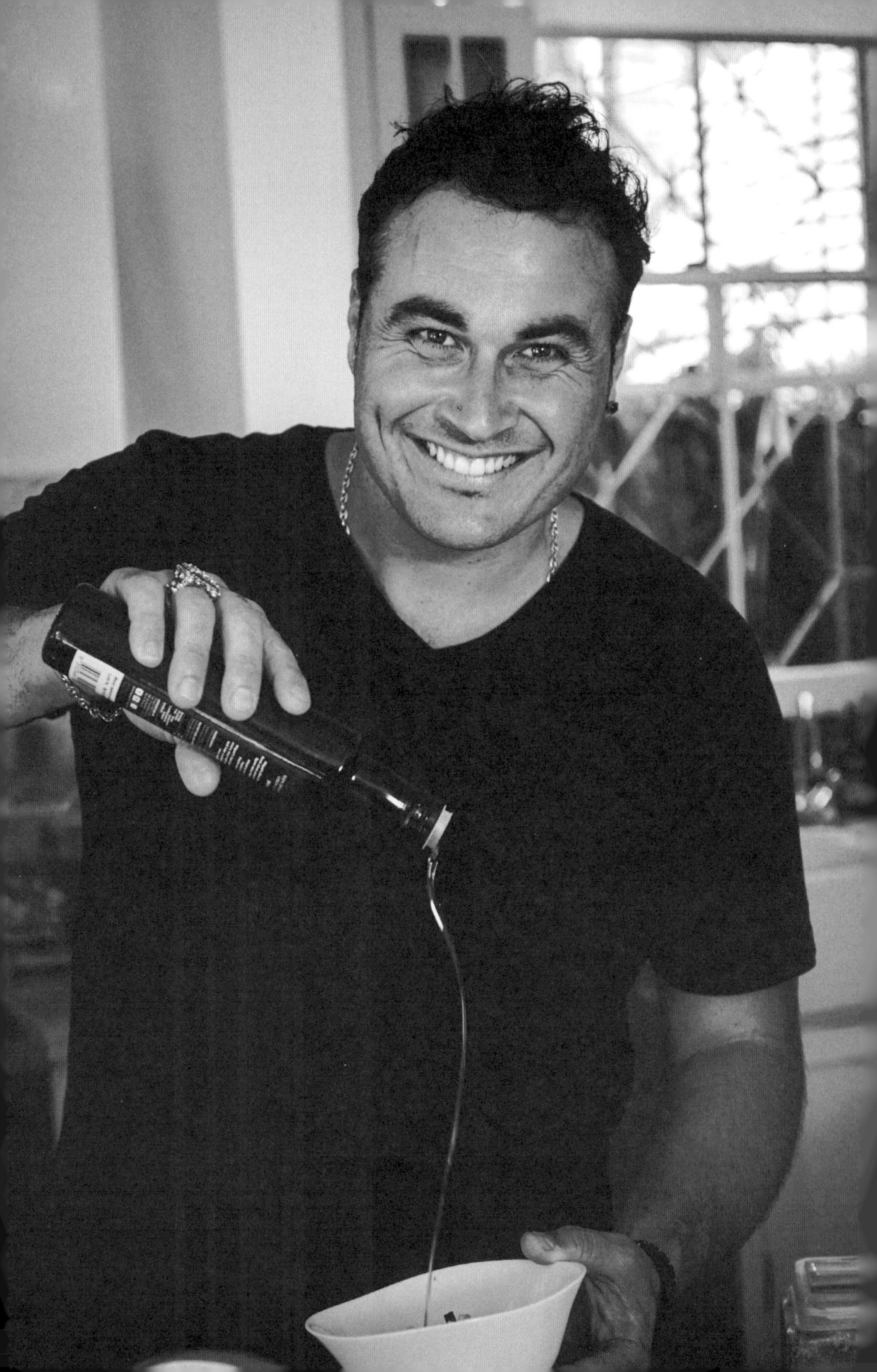

YOGHURT FLATBREAD

Making your own flatbread and dips results in a great sense of achievement and will definitely impress everyone. Something so simple like yoghurt and flour can make the most delicious freshly grilled bread without having to wait or prove the dough; there are no complications, just a hot barbecue grill to get those special grill marks Using sweet potato and beetroot for the hummus is a little more unusual but the flavours are outstanding.

Makes 12

500g self raising flour
500g Greek yoghurt
6 stems fresh thyme (leaves only)
2 stems fresh rosemary (leaves only)
salt
olive oil
extra flour for dusting the bench and kneading the dough
lemon wedges, to serve

Put the flour in a big mixing bowl and make a well in the centre. Add the yoghurt to the well. These are the two ingredients that will make your bread.

Next add the flavourings: season with salt and add fresh thyme, rosemary and a splash of olive oil. You can experiment with alternative herb flavours in this step if you prefer.

Mix with your hands until the dough is combined. If the dough is too dry, add more yoghurt. If it is too wet, add more flour.

Flour your work surface and knead the ball of dough with your hands until it becomes a nice ball.

Divide into six portions and roll each one into a flat circle, pizza thick, with a rolling pin. Brush with olive oil and grill on a medium barbecue for about 4 minutes until you get lovely grill marks. You could also use a skillet on the stovetop to similar effect.

To serve, slice each bread in half and arrange the yoghurt bread on a platter or wooden board with dips and lemon wedges.

HIGHER PROTEIN • SOFTER OPTION • HIGHER FIBRE • LOW SPICE

BEETROOT AND CUMIN HUMMUS WITH TOASTED PECANS

Serves 8

200g canned chickpeas, drained and rinsed
2 tbsp tahini
2 cloves garlic, crushed
1 small knob (the size of half a thumb) ginger, peeled and chopped
juice of 1 lemon
1 large roasted beetroot peeled, or 150g tin roasted beetroots drained
1½ tsp ground cumin
½ tsp Spanish paprika
sea salt & cracked black pepper

TO SERVE
handful of pecans, toasted and chopped
extra virgin olive oil
natural Greek yoghurt

Place all the ingredients in a food processor and process until creamy.

To serve, scatter over pecan chunks and drizzle with olive oil and a generous dollop of Greek yoghurt.

EASIEST SWEET POTATO HUMMUS

Serves 8

500g sweet potato, peeled and chopped into chunks
1 tbsp tahini
3 small garlic cloves, minced
1 tsp Spanish paprika, plus extra for seasoning
½ lemon, zested and juiced
3 tbsp extra virgin olive oil, plus extra to drizzle
½ bunch chives, finely chopped
1 tbsp sesame seeds

To make the dip put the sweet potato in a medium saucepan filled with cold, salted water. Place on the stove, bring to the boil then cook for 15–20 minutes or until soft. Drain well then mash with a fork.

Add the tahini, garlic, paprika, lemon zest and juice and mix well. Gradually stir in the olive oil.

Garnish with chives and sesame seeds.

TUNA AND WASABI FRESH CUCUMBER CANNELLONI

Roll baby roll, the easiest cooking technique in the world – refreshing, nutritious and very easy to make. These cylindric parcels of goodness will become a family favourite.

Makes 6 rolls

1½ avocados
1 tsp wasabi paste
10 leaves fresh basil
1 tsp lime juice
1 clove garlic
salt & pepper
1 English cucumber
2 tbsp smashed wasabi peas
1 tin of good quality tuna or good quality sardines (approx. 185g)
1 small punnet seaweed sesame salad

Blend the avocado, wasabi, basil, lime juice, garlic and salt in a food processor or blender until smooth.

Use a mandolin or potato peeler to cut long thin strips from the cucumber.

Spread a thin layer of the avocado mixture along the length of the cucumber strips, and then top with a sprinkle of crushed wasabi peas.

Ensure you get avocado mixture all the way to the end of each strip, which will help to stick the roll together. Place a chunk of fish in the middle then roll up.

Top with seaweed salad.

LIFE FORCE

ROASTED VEGETABLE SALAD

Roasted vegetables are soooo delicious! When you roast a vegetable, it is pretty much like turning up the volume of its flavour. This is a very generous salad that is perfect for the whole family. My favourite part is using the juices from the roasting tray for dressing and marking the Brussels sprouts to give them that beautiful caramelised look that very posh restaurants do. Serve with your favourite protein for a nourishing meal. The secret to roasting veggies is to cut them smaller so they cook faster and the original flavour is preserved.

Serves 6

olive oil
10 Brussels sprouts, halved
10 shallots, peeled and halved
½ Kent pumpkin, skin on, sliced into thin wedges
5 golden baby beetroots, halved
5 purple baby beetroots, halved
1 bunch of baby kale
½ bunch of sage
½ bunch of rosemary
½ bunch of thyme
salt & pepper

DRESSING

1 tbsp Dijon mustard
juices from roasting tray
2 tbsp extra virgin olive oil
juice of half a lemon

TO SERVE

1 handful of walnuts, toasted
2 tbsp crumbled feta
5 baby radishes, thinly sliced (optional for garnish)

Preheat oven to 200°C.

Heat 1 tbsp olive oil in a saucepan over a high heat. Sear the Brussels sprouts and shallot halves in the hot pan, giving them a nice colour on the cut surface. This is called 'marking' and gives a nice crunch and flavor to the vegetables.

Combine the sprouts, shallots, pumpkin wedges, beetroots, baby kale and herbs in a roasting tray. Season with salt and pepper and drizzle generously with olive oil. Roast in the oven for 20–30 minutes, until vegetables are cooked through.

For the dressing, combine all ingredients with juices from the roasting tray in a screw-top jar and shake until well combined.

Transfer the roasted vegetables to a serving platter and sprinkle with walnuts, feta and sliced radishes, if using. Drizzle with the dressing. Serve warm.

HIGHER FIBRE

BARRY DU BOIS & MIGUEL MAESTRE

LIFE FORCE

PAN CON TOMATE

The most famous tapa in every city of Spain, the unique and humble pan con tomate – tomato bread – is something magic that happens when you grate a tomato ... the best tomato flesh gets separated from the skin but keeps all the flavour. The rubbing of the fresh garlic clove is something that has been happening in every Spanish home for centuries ... it is the perfect example that the simple things in life are the best, and how the Mediterranean way of eating is humble, delicious and true to the ingredients, making it so exceptional and enjoyable.

The anchovies and ham are optional – Baz craves very salty food due to his treatment and these ingredients have a salty flavour profile.

Makes 6 tapas

2 ripe field tomatoes at room temperature
generous drizzle of good quality extra virgin olive oil
salt & pepper
thick sourdough, sliced and grilled or toasted
1 garlic clove, peeled and halved
6 white anchovies or 6 slices of ham – Spanish of course!
½ bunch finely chopped chives

This recipe is so simple! To start, grate the tomatoes using a box grater (discarding the skin) over a mixing bowl, add a splash of olive oil and season with salt and pepper.

To assemble, rub the garlic on each slice of the bread then spoon the tomatoes on top and drizzle with olive oil. Top with white anchovies or ham (if using), a splash of olive oil and chives and you're done. Too easy.

BARRY DU BOIS & MIGUEL MAESTRE

SPANISH TORTILLA DE PATATAS

My mum Florentina makes the best tortilla de patatas in the world. She used to make it when we were little and use like 30 eggs in one time. It was supposed to last for a few days, but we couldn't walk pass the fridge without the temptation of opening the door and having a slice – the best snack ever, perfect in a sandwich or just by itself. It is one of my greatest memories of cooking and I love that I can share it. Just remember to cook it perfectly is the best tip … it is all in the turning … don't think about it just go for it.

Serves 6

5 eggs
60ml olive oil
1 large potato, peeled and cut into 1cm slices
3 small brown onions, thinly sliced
3 garlic cloves, thinly sliced
salt & pepper
2 handfuls English spinach
2 tbsp toasted walnuts
a splash of olive oil
lemon wedges, to serve

Break the eggs into a medium bowl. Whisk lightly to just break yolks.

Heat oil in a medium (20cm) non-stick frying pan.

Add the potato, onion and garlic. Cook over a medium heat, turning occasionally, until the potato is tender and the onion is soft, then remove from heat. Strain oil from the pan and stir this mixture into the eggs. Season.

Increase heat. Return mixture to frying pan when smoky hot.

Reduce to a low heat and cook on one side for about 4 minutes or until just set. Invert tortilla onto a plate then slide it back into the pan to cook the other side. Cook for a further 4 minutes.

In a mortar and pestle (or food processor) work the spinach and walnuts with a splash of olive oil drizzled on top until a pesto consistency.

Serve tortilla with spinach, walnut pesto and lemon wedges on the side.

HIGHER PROTEIN • SOFTER OPTION • LOW SPICE - omit pepper

LIFE FORCE

SUPER GREEN QUESADILLA, THE NEW MEXICAN SUPERHERO

Quesadilla is a great meal to share, and is very easy to cook. This Mexican delight has Spanish influences, and originally was just made with cheese, and following that with meat, but nowadays we can add beautiful things like delicious veggies.

The perfect way to cook them is in a frying pan with dry heat so they crisp up outside and the cheese is melted inside. Cut them into triangles almost like pizza slices and top them with dressing and salad.

Makes 4

1 avocado
juice of 1 lime
sea salt
1 tbsp olive oil
2 spring onions, green only, finely sliced
1 zucchini, grated
4 Brussels sprouts, thinly shredded
handful of baby spinach leaves
½ cup edamame beans, rinsed and strained
1 tsp mild Mexican seasoning
4 large green tortillas
¼ bunch of mint, leaves picked
¼ bunch of coriander
½ cup grated mozzarella
½ cup grated tasty cheese

CABBAGE SALAD

2 tbsp apple cider vinegar
1 tbsp extra virgin olive oil
pinch of salt
pinch of Mexican seasoning
½ green cabbage, thinly shredded
250g mixed coloured cherry tomatoes, quartered (green is preferable)
handful of spinach
60ml Greek yoghurt, to serve
pinch salt

Save a quarter of the avocado for the dressing then mash the rest with the lime juice and salt.

Heat a large frying pan over a high heat. Sauté the onion, zucchini, and sprouts for 3 minutes in the oil until the onions soften.

Add the spinach leaves, beans and seasoning and cook for a further minute until heated through.

Take a green tortilla, covering the base with avocado mash. Then add a quarter of the bean mixture to the tortilla to cover half of the tortilla. Top with picked mint and coriander leaves and sprinkle with a quarter of the cheese.

Preheat another pan – there is no need to add any oil. Transfer the tortilla to the pan and heat for one minute. Fold the tortilla in half and cook for 2–3 minutes until the tortilla begins to colour, flip the tortilla over and cook for a further 2 minutes until the cheese has completely melted. Repeat with the remaining tortillas.

Whilst the tortillas are cooking, prepare the salad.

Mix the vinegar and olive oil in a large salad bowl. Add a pinch of salt and a pinch of Mexican seasoning. Add the shredded cabbage and tomatoes and toss to coat with dressing.

Blend the spinach and yogurt with a splash of olive oil and the reserved quarter of avocado until smooth.

Take the tortilla off the heat and cut into quarters. Serve with a dollop of green yoghurt and the cabbage salad.
GREEN GREEN GREEN!

LIFE FORCE

SWEET POTATO AND BLACK ANGUS BEEF FILLET COTTAGE PIE

A cottage pie has the greatness of being pastry-free, making it a very easy dish to make. My favourite part is the mouth-watering soft beef tenderloin and the little caramelised peaks of sweet potato mash which feel almost crispy. A big spoonful of this pie, with the meat and the mash together, is almost the perfect meal.

HIGHER PROTEIN • SOFTER OPTION • HIGHER FIBRE • LOW SPICE - omit chilli & pepper

Serves 8

600g beef angus fillet tail, sliced into finger-thick medallions
2 tbsp plain flour
salt & pepper
2 tbsp extra virgin olive oil
2 brown onions, diced
1 leek, diced
3 sticks celery, diced
2 carrots, diced
400g tin chopped tomatoes
250ml chicken stock
1 tbsp tomato paste
2 tbsp Worcestershire sauce
1 chilli
⅓ bunch thyme, leaves only
3 sweet potatoes
50g butter
50ml light cream

Preheat the oven to 180°C.

Dust the beef with flour and season with salt and pepper.

Sear the meat in a large saucepan with olive oil on a low heat until browned (be careful not to burn the flour). Set aside.

In the same pan cook the onions, leek, celery and carrots until soft. Add the tinned tomatoes, chicken stock, tomato paste, Worcestershire sauce, chilli and thyme. Mix well and bring to the boil. Add meat and set aside.

POTATO TOPPING:

To make the potato topping, peel the sweet potatoes, boil until tender then mash with butter and cream. Using a piping bag with a star nozzle, top the pie with sweet potato mixture creating your own design.

Bake in the oven until topping is golden brown, which should take about 20–30 min.

MOROCCAN CHICKEN

One-pot wonders are one of the smartest ways to cook as everything goes in the same pot and all the flavours mix together. The juices from the chicken help the veggies to achieve extra flavour. In Morocco, ras al hanout means 'the best in the shop', or the best spices available. You always can add more or less depending on how spicy you like your dishes.

It is better to use chicken thighs rather than breast as the thighs have a much better flavour and cooking on the bone prevents the meat from becoming dry; rather, it stays succulent and moist.

Couscous is the perfect garnish and the secret to cooking it is to make sure the steam stays in the bowl, so keep the plastic wrap super-tight

Serves 6

- 3 cloves garlic, peeled and chopped
- 2 tbsp chopped coriander roots and stems
- salt & pepper
- 2 tbsp extra virgin olive oil
- 1½ tbsp honey
- 1 tbsp lemon juice, plus wedges to serve
- 3 tsp ras el hanout (Moroccan seasoning)
- 4 chicken thighs, skin on, bone in
- 1 bunch Dutch carrots, washed and trimmed, halved lengthways
- ½ small cauliflower, cut into florets
- 1 red capsicum, seeds removed, cut into 2cm thick slices
- 2 tsp cumin seeds

COUSCOUS

- 1½ cups couscous
- 2 tsp unsalted butter
- 2 tsp extra virgin olive oil
- ¼ cup pistachios, toasted, chopped
- ¼ cup chopped green olives
- ¼ cup currants
- ½ cup coriander leaves, torn

Preheat the oven to 200°C.

In a mortar and pestle, pound the garlic, coriander roots and stems and a large pinch of salt to a paste. Add 1 tbsp each of the olive oil and honey, lemon juice and ras el hanout. Season with black pepper and mix well.

Place the chicken in a bowl and pour over the marinade. Using your hands, massage the marinade into the flesh. Set aside.

Place the carrots, cauliflower, capsicum and 1 tablespoon olive oil in a baking dish and season to taste. Toss the vegetables until well coated. Drizzle with the remaining honey, scatter over the cumin seeds and arrange the chicken pieces on top, drizzling any remaining marinade over the chicken.

Transfer the baking dish to the oven and cook for 30–35 minutes until the chicken is golden and cooked through and the vegetables are tender. Remove from the oven and rest for 5 minutes.

Meanwhile, place the couscous and butter in a bowl and season with salt and pepper. Pour in 375ml boiling water and stir for 30 seconds with a fork. Cover and set aside for 10 minutes until the water has been absorbed. Stir with a fork to fluff the grains. Add the remaining ingredients and toss until well combined.

To serve, divide the couscous and vegetables between plates. Top with chicken and spoon over some of the baking juices from the chicken. Serve with lemon wedges.

HIGHER PROTEIN • SOFTER OPTION - omit nuts

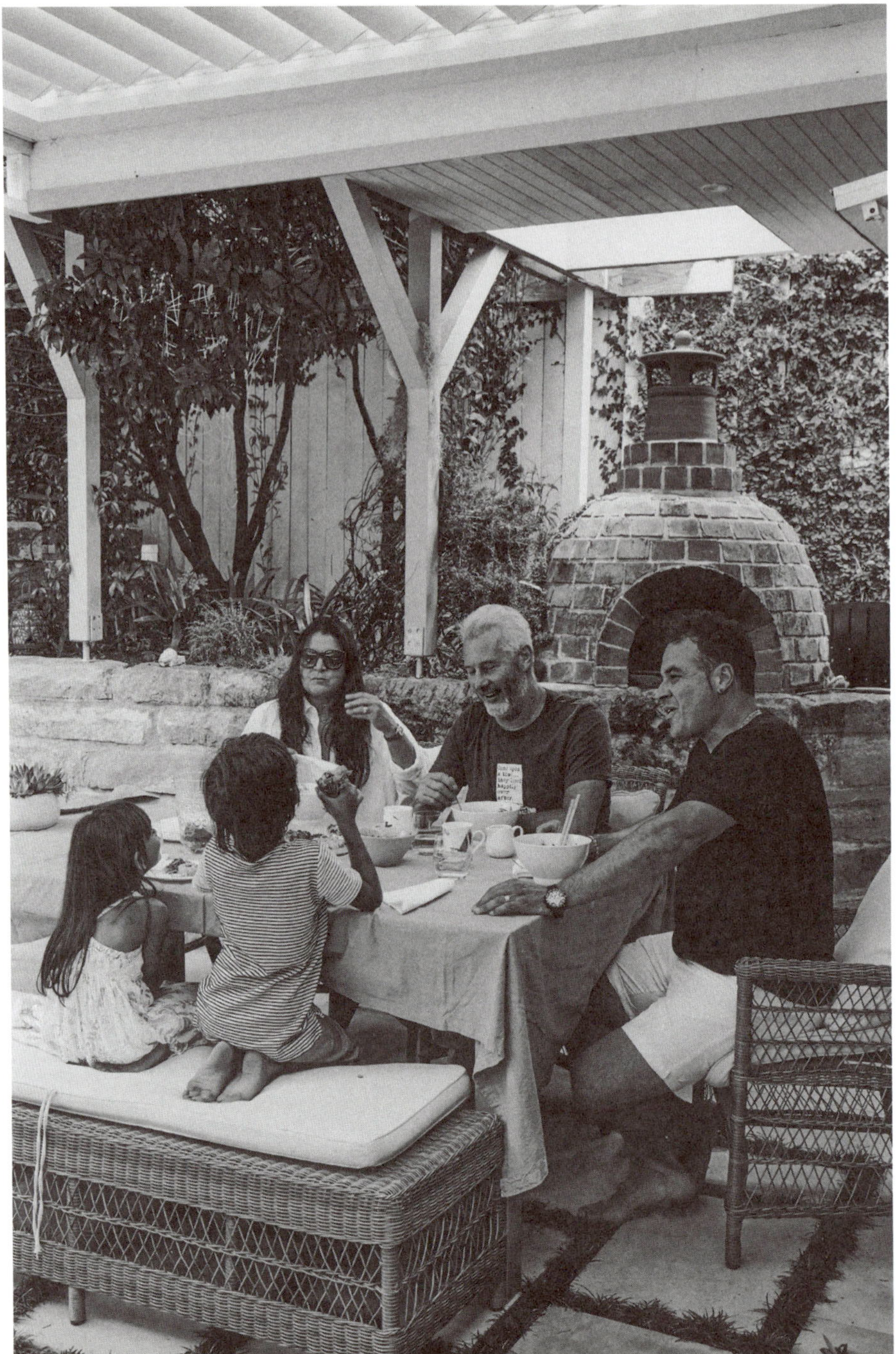

LAMB AND SPINACH GOZLEME-AND-YOU

My favourite food in the markets is always a gozleme. I love watching the Turkish ladies making them to order. This is a great recipe that embodies a real authentic Turkish experience. The secret is to allow the dough to rise as much as possible until it is double its size

Serves 8

1 x 7g sachet instant dried yeast
1 tsp caster sugar
1 tsp salt
290ml luke-warm water
450g plain flour
2 tbsp hot paprika
80ml extra virgin olive oil
4 lamb fillets
salt & pepper
200g feta
100g baby spinach
lemon wedges (to serve)

To make the dough, combine the yeast, sugar, salt and 90 ml of the water in a small bowl and mix. Set aside for 10 minutes until it begins to bubble.

In a large bowl stir 1 tablespoon of paprika into the flour then make a well in the centre. Add the yeast mixture, olive oil and the remaining water. Working from the centre, slowly mix to incorporate the flour, stirring until a rough dough starts to form. Turn out onto a lightly floured surface and knead for 10 minutes until smooth and elastic. Place the dough in a lightly oiled bowl and set aside, covered, for 45 minutes until doubled in size.

Meanwhile, heat a barbecue plate until very hot. Place the lamb in a bowl with the remaining paprika and season to taste. Lightly oil the hotplate and cook the lamb for 2–3 minutes until just cooked through. Set aside until cool, then thinly slice. Reduce the temperature to medium.

Divide the dough into 4 and roll each piece into a rectangle about 20cm x 30cm. Layer the lamb along one half of each piece of dough. Crumble the feta over the lamb and top with spinach. Fold the dough in half and pinch the edges together to seal.

Brush each gozleme lightly with oil and cook for 3–4 minutes on each side until golden. Remove from the heat, cut into quarters and serve with lemon wedges.

HIGHER PROTEIN • SOFTER OPTION • LOW SPICE - omit pepper/paprika

LIFE FORCE

FLATHEAD FISH TACOS

Tacos must be the most ingenious finger food ever invented. There is nothing better than the soft tortilla to hold the delicious flatty fillets, with the freshness of the corn and the crunch of the cabbage … it is the most relaxing meal ever, street food at its best. I remember being in Los Angeles with Baz and eating so many from the food trucks and listening to all his fascinating stories about when he was a young man. Baz has the most amazing stories about life he is so good at sharing them. Sometimes I might think, 'I heard that story before, Baz,' but he is so excited that I won't stop him and I hear it again … Well, that's what friends are for.

Makes 6 tacos

¼ red cabbage, finely shredded
½ iceberg lettuce, finely shredded
1 carrot, peeled, finely sliced or grated
2 watermelon radishes, shaved with a mandolin
1 garlic clove, peeled and finely sliced
2 avocados
2 limes
6 flathead fish fillets
2 corn cobs
1 tbsp of chipotle sauce
½ bunch chives, chopped
3 vine tomatoes, diced
salt & pepper
6 soft round tortillas, warmed

Combine the cabbage, lettuce, carrot, radish and garlic in a bowl.

Cut the avocados in half and remove the stones. Squeeze lime juice over each half and use a fork to mash until smooth.

Heat an oiled pan over a medium heat; cook the fish fillets for 2–3 minutes each side. Remove from the pan and place on a plate. Place the pan back over the heat.

For the salsa, cut the corn kernels from the cob and place in a pan, add the chipotle sauce, chives and tomatoes. Cook, stirring for 3–5 minutes or until tomatoes just start to break down. Season with salt and pepper.

Place the warmed tortillas on a clean, dry, flat surface. Spread each one with avocado, spoon over the salsa, top with fish and a handful of salad. Serve.

HIGHER PROTEIN • HIGHER FIBRE • LOW SPICE - omit chipotle & pepper

SPANISH RICE-CRUSTED SARDINES, FULL OF BEANS ON RYE WITH CRASHED NOT SMASHED AVOCADO

Spending time talking to Barry has been a very important part of understanding his favourite flavours – he is in love with sardines and, guess what, so am I! As a Spaniard, I grew up eating them as a snack, and crusting them with rice (Spanish white rice, if you can!) brings them to the next level, just make sure the crust is very fine to achieve a wonderful crunch. This is a Spanish delicacy that is perfect to share.

Serves 4

50g white rice
25g plain or wholemeal flour
2 tbsp water
salt & pepper
8 fresh butterflied sardines
1 tbsp olive oil
100g edamame beans, thinly sliced
100g giant lima beans cooked
½ bunch parsley, finely chopped
2 garlic cloves, minced
1 avocado
olive oil
salt
lemon juice
rye bread thick sliced
lemon wedges, to serve

Using a coffee grinder or mortar and pestle, grind the rice to a coarse powder. Place on a plate.

Whisk the flour and water in a small bowl to form a smooth batter. Season.

Pat sardines dry with absorbent paper. Dip skin-side only in batter, then dip both sides into powdered rice.

Heat oil in a non-stick frying pan.

Cook the sardines on medium heat, skin-side down, for about 4 minutes or until crust is crisp and golden. Turn and cook for about a further 30 seconds. Drain on absorbent paper.

Add edamame and lima beans to the same clean pan with a splash of olive oil. Cook over a medium heat, stirring occasionally for 2 minutes until lightly browned. Stir in parsley and garlic. Season to taste.

In a medium-size bowl, crash the avocado using a fork with a splash of olive oil, pinch of salt and a squeeze of lemon juice.

To serve, cover toasted rye bread with crashed avocado, then beans and top with sardines. Include lemon wedges on the side.

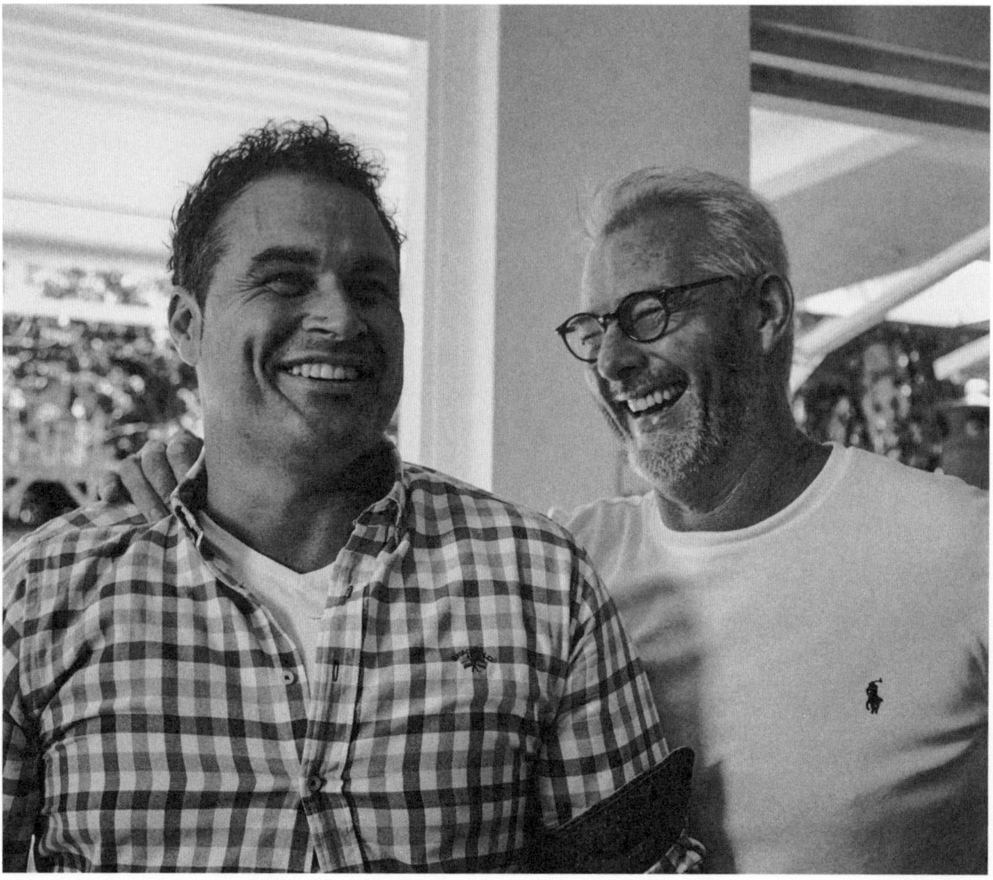

CRISPY SKIN BARRAMUNDI CHIMICHURRI

This is the perfect way to get a crispy skin every time … the secret is to properly dry the moisture in the skin, and then score the side of the skin so the heat cooks the fish gently. The paper on the pan helps to avoid sticking – most annoying – and it is the best when the fish has crispy skin which is soooo nice to eat, almost like pork crackling.

Serves 2

2 x 200g barramundi fillets, skin-on
2 teaspoons olive oil
sea salt & pepper

CHIMICHURRI
1 bunch fresh coriander, roughly chopped, roots included
2 handful baby spinach
5 cloves garlic
1 pink eshallot, finely chopped
1 bunch chives, roughly chopped
½ bunch fresh oregano leaves
2 green chilies
1 tbsp red wine vinegar
juice of 1 lime
½ cup olive oil

Pat the fish dry with paper towel and score the skin with a sharp knife. Season.

Cut out a piece of greaseproof paper to fit in the bottom of your fry pan.

Heat oil in a pan over medium heat. If too high the skin will burn before the fish is cooked.

Place the paper into the pan and immediately place the barramundi fillets, skin side down onto the paper.

Press the fish into the pan with an egg flip or saucepan lid to ensure maximum crispness, and prevent it from curling up. Giving skin 100 percent contact with the heat of the pan will ensure it's crisp.

The fish should remain skin side down for 90 percent of the cooking time (around 7 minutes). As the fish cooks (the sides of the fillet will change to a bright white colour), baste the fillet with a bit of butter and its own juices.

Flip the fillet over and cook for another minute. Remove from heat.

To make the chimichurri, in a large mortar and pestle, grind the ingredients together, adding the oil and lime gradually until a chunky consistency.

The longer it stays in the fridge the better it will taste, but do eat it within 3 days.

Serve the fish with chimichurri and a side of cooked white rice (¾ cup per person).

HIGHER PROTEIN • SOFTER OPTION - remove skin • HIGHER FIBRE

LIFE FORCE

BLACK SKIN ROASTED MUSHROOM CHICKEN

This is a very different approach to the traditional roasted chicken. The mushrooms have a high water content that is released while roasting and prevents the chicken from drying out. The presentation is pretty spectacular.

Make sure you separate the skin from the flesh very carefully and push the mushroom butter all over under the skin. The stuffing is a perfect garnish and cooks with all the chicken juices in the process of roasting.

HIGHER PROTEIN • SOFTER OPTION • HIGHER FIBRE • LOW SPICE - omit paprika & chorizo

Serves 6

20g unsalted butter, softened
2 punnets chestnut mushrooms, finely chopped in food processor
3 sprigs thyme, leaves picked
1 large chicken, around 2.5kg
1 tsp Spanish smoky paprika
1 lemon

STUFFING
1 tbsp olive oil
2 fresh cured chorizo sausages, small diced
4 medium flat mushrooms
4 spring onions, chopped

VEGETABLES
1 bunch baby beets, washed and halved (golden and purple)
1 bunch Dutch carrots, washed and trimmed (purple, yellow, orange)
1 bunch spring onions, trimmed
2 bulbs baby fennel, quartered

Preheat oven to 180°C. Mix the butter, chopped mushroom and thyme together and season generously with salt and pepper.

Gently loosen the skin of the chicken by pushing your fingers along the surface of the meat around the breast and thighs. Push the butter under the skin and work the butter as far down under the skin as possible.

Sprinkle the paprika over the skin and rub until evenly coated.

FOR THE STUFFING:

Heat the olive oil in a large frying pan over medium-high heat. Add the chorizo, mushroom and spring onion and cook for 2 minutes, stirring regularly.

Season to taste and remove from the heat.

Stuff the chicken cavity with the field mushrooms and chorizo sauté, pressing firmly so it roasts with the chicken juices, and close up with the lemon.

Chop veggies and place into the base of a baking tray. The beetroot can be cooked whole or halved. Season the veggies with lots of salt and pepper, then drizzle with olive oil and mix together using your hands.

Cook the veggies together with the chicken, allowing 30 minutes cooking per 500g of chicken.

Serve with stuffing, slaw salad and veggies.

FISH AND SWEET POTATO PAPRIKA CHIPS WITH TARTARE SAUCE

My favourite part of fish and chips … fresh fish, crispy crunch and the best chips. Allow me to show you a way to obtain all these things without having to go through the oily avenue of frying. Pan-fry the fish to perfection with the perfect fish (snapper) and use a quirky way to add the crunch, saving time and effort and, of course, giving the sweet potato chips a nice touch of Spain in that hot oven … yesss, or (better) síííí, 'paprika'!

Serves 4-6

SWEET POTATO WEDGES
1 large sweet potato, cut into wedges
1½ tbsp olive oil
1 tbsp smoked Spanish paprika
salt

TARTARE SAUCE
½ cup Japanese mayonnaise or Greek yoghurt
1 tbsp baby capers, chopped finely
6 cornichons, finely diced
1 bunch dill, finely chopped
¼ Spanish onion, finely diced

CRUMB
2 cups panko crumbs, pan fried in ½ tbsp olive oil until golden brown
½ cup toasted and salted macadamias, crushed
1 tbsp dried oregano
zest of 1 lemon
salt & pepper

FISH
2 x 200g snapper fillets, cut into thick fish fingers
1 tbsp butter
1 tbsp olive oil
salt & pepper

Preheat the oven to 240°C.

Toss sweet potato wedges in olive oil and smoked paprika. Season generously. Spread on a lined baking tray and roast for 25–30 minutes until crispy and cooked through.

Meanwhile, make the tartare sauce by mixing the mayonnaise, capers, cornichons, dill and onion.

To make the crumb, mix the panko, crushed macadamias, dried oregano and lemon zest together. Season with salt and pepper.

Approximately 5 minutes before the sweet potato is cooked, heat oil and butter in a frying pan. Cook the snapper fillet, basting it with the melted butter/oil mixture until cooked through.

Remove cooked fish from the pan, brush with the tartare sauce and press gently into breadcrumb mixture to coat.

Serve hot with sweet potato wedges.

HIGHER PROTEIN • LOW SPICE - omit pepper/paprika

LIFE FORCE

OKONOMIYAKI OF SALMON AND SALSA VERDE

Best breakfast, lunch or dinner ever! The crunch of cabbage through the pancake makes it feel sooo delicious. This is a great base for any of your favourite ingredients as you can use any type of fish or meat and cook it in the hotplate next to the pancake, so all of those lovely flavours are together in the hotplate at the same time. The salsa verde is a great garnish for it and makes the salmon soooo tasty; you can use crispy shallots if you can't find bonito flakes (they are often found in the Asian section of supermarkets).

HIGHER PROTEIN • SOFTER OPTION • HIGHER FIBRE • LOW SPICE - omit chilli

Serves 2

50g fresh skinless salmon fillet, cut in thin slices sashimi-style
2 tbsp crumbled feta
1 soft boiled egg (6 min and straight to ice water)
bonito flakes to garnish
coriander leaves, to garnish

PANCAKE
80g plain flour
120ml water
2 eggs
200g shredded cabbage (green and red)
3 spring onions, green part only, thinly sliced

SALSA VERDE
2 garlic cloves
1 long red chilli
juice of ½ lemon
½ cup parsley leaves
½ cup coriander leaves
4 tbsp olive oil

For the pancake, mix the flour, water and eggs to a smooth consistency, then fold in the rest of the ingredients and mix well together.

Pour into a pan or onto a barbecue hot plate, using a scraper to shape it into a large circle about 20cm in diameter. Cook for 5 minutes, allowing the water and cabbage to steam with the heat. When there is a crust on the bottom, flip to cook the pancake on the other side for another 5 minutes.

While the pancake is cooking, sear the salmon for 1 minute on each side.

Meanwhile make the salsa verde by blending garlic, chilli, lemon juice, parsley, coriander and olive oil. Season to taste.

When pancake and salmon are cooked, top pancake with crumble feta. Drizzle with 2 tablespoons of salsa verde and soft boiled egg cut in quarters with a sprinkle of bonito flakes. Serve immediately.

BARRY DU BOIS & MIGUEL MAESTRE

LIFE FORCE

CORN AND ZUCCHINI MINI HOTCAKES

Zucchini and corn are in every menu in Australia, but how can we get the best out of both ingredients to maximize their flavour profile? Grating the fresh corn is amazing as we get all the flesh and we leave the skins behind. What's more, the pure, bright yellow colour of corn gives the hotcakes a really sunny touch. The trick with the zucchini is to use a spiralizer or mandolin to get the thinnest slices you can, and then add them to the batter just before you spoon the mixture into the hot pan in order to preserve the fresh zucchini flavour.

Serves 6

1½ cups plain spelt or wholemeal flour
1 tbsp flaxseed
50g Manchego cheese, finely grated
salt & pepper
½ bunch chives, roughly chopped
1 cup full fat milk, extra milk may be required
2 free-range organic eggs
3 corn cobs
3 zucchinis
extra virgin olive oil
1 block Haloumi, thickly sliced
rocket leaves, to serve
beetroot hummus, to serve
lemon wedges, to serve

To make the batter, place the flour, flaxseed and Manchego in a large bowl, season with salt and pepper and mix well with clean hands. Add the chives.

Combine the milk and eggs in a small bowl and whisk; pour into the flour mixture gradually and mix to make a thick batter the consistency of creamy mash. You can add extra milk if needed.

Grate the corn into the bowl and mix well. Discard the husks.

Using a mandolin or spiralizer, finely cut the zucchinis into thin strips.

Heat an oiled frying pan over a medium heat.

Using two spoons, take a golf ball sized amount of the zucchini and place into the batter to coat, then place your mini hotcake into the frying pan and cook for 2–3 minutes until golden underneath. Turn and cook a further 1–2 minutes until cooked through. Continue with the remaining zucchini and batter to cook in batches.

Fry the haloumi slices in the frying pan for 30 seconds each side until golden.

To serve, spoon the beetroot hummus onto a plate, top with a little rocket, add a hotcake, and a slice of haloumi, then another fritter, with a lemon wedge on the side. Perfect with soft boiled eggs (which I make by boiling for 6 minutes and then plunging them immediately into iced water).

PEARL BARLEY AND MUSHROOM RISOTTO

Pearl barley has an amazing texture and is a match made in heaven with mushrooms; this combination is fantastic. The secret to achieving the ultimate mushroom flavour is the mushroom stock in which we cook the barley. Using olive oil and butter together caramelises the mushroom beautifully as the butter doesn't burn and we still get that lovely nutty flavour.

Serves 4-6

30g packet dried porcini mushrooms
250g pearl barley
2 sprigs thyme
salt & pepper
40g butter
1 tbsp extra virgin olive oil
2 onions, finely chopped
2 garlic cloves, crushed
300g mixed mushrooms, plus extra to serve
20ml light cream
50g grated pecorino, to serve
baby rocket, to serve
lemon wedge, to serve

Bring 1 litre of water to the boil in a saucepan. Add the dried mushrooms, pearl barley and thyme and season well with salt. Reduce the heat to a steady simmer and cook for 15 minutes until the barley is just tender. Strain, reserving the barley mixture and stock separately.

Heat the butter and olive oil in a large frying pan over medium heat. Add the onion and garlic and cook until soft and starting to caramelise. Tear three quarters of the mushrooms into pieces and add to the frying pan. Cook, stirring regularly, for 2–3 minutes or until the mushrooms begin to soften. Add the barley and enough of the stock to almost cover the mushrooms. Simmer for 2–3 minutes until the mushrooms are cooked and the liquid has reduced and thickened. Stir in the cream and simmer until heated through.

Remove from the heat, stir through the pecorino, remaining mushrooms and season to taste. Spoon into bowls and top with rocket. Serve with lemon wedges.

SOFTER OPTION • HIGHER FIBRE • LOW SPICE

LIFE FORCE

BARBECUED SWORDFISH NIÇOISE WITH BASIL, CAPER AND LEMON

I remember Baz talking to me about his cravings for salty food, such as capers and anchovies ... this nicoise is the perfect scenario to get the best from the ocean and the best from the land. It's full of crunch from delicious veggies, plus the bread and potatoes make it very filling. Topped with a delicious grilled fish, this may just become your new favourite dish.

Serves 4

SALAD
1 olive baguette
2 tablespoons olive oil
300g mixed beans (green, sugar snaps, yellow), ends trimmed
1 sweet potato roasted and cut in cubes
15 manzanilla olives stuffed with feta
1 punnet heirloom tomatoes, halved
1 tablespoon sherry vinegar
1 teaspoon wholegrain mustard
1 teaspoon honey
2 x 150g swordfish steaks (you can use trout as well)
1 baby cos lettuce, roughly chopped
1 lime, cut into wedges, to serve

BASIL, CAPER AND LEMON DRESSING
1 cup torn basil leaves
2 tablespoons chives
2 anchovies
1 teaspoon capers
juice of 1 lemon
3 tablespoons extra-virgin olive oil
salt & pepper

SWORDFISH
To serve

Cut baguette into 2cm croutons – you want approximately 1 cup. Heat olive oil in a large frying pan on medium-high heat. Add croutons to pan, sprinkle with salt and toast until lightly golden, 2–3 minutes. Set aside to cool on paper towels.

To make the dressing, place basil leaves, chives, anchovies, capers, lemon juice, olive oil and a teaspoon of water in a food processor or blender. Pulse until smooth, season to taste with salt and pepper.

Cook beans in a saucepan of boiling water for 2–3 minutes. Drain, refresh in cold water, drain again. Toss with the sweet potato, olives, tomatoes and half the dressing (reserve the remaining dressing). Stir through vinegar, mustard and honey.

Pat fish dry with paper towels, remove any remaining scales or bones and rub with reserved dressing. Heat a drizzle of oil in a chargrill pan (or barbecue grill) on medium to high heat and cook fish for 1–2 minutes each side or until just cooked through.

To serve, scatter lettuce and croutons over plates, top with salad and swordfish. Serve lime wedges on the side.

HIGHER PROTEIN • HIGHER FIBRE

PAELLA A LA MAESTRE

This is my signature dish. Maestre is the name of my mum's family, and this dish as such has defined my life as a chef at every level. It is what I love to cook the most, perfect for sharing, full of passion, full of colour, full of flavour and defines what cooking means to me – SHARING.

You can have a paella for two people to 100,000 people (the biggest one ever cooked), but you cannot have a paella for one … this dish is designed to be shared. I remember cooking a massive paella at Barry's place one Christmas party and the food became the entertainment as everyone got involved.

I have cooked it many times with Chris, Amanda and Baz, and Amanda is now a paella queen – she cooks it for everyone at her dinner parties.

Cooking from the heart is contagious and I hope everyone who cooks this recipe for the people they love can feel the same reward that I feel every time I make it.

Serves 6

250g diced white fish snapper, dory, barra, flathead or cod
8 king prawns, peeled
200g baby calamari, cleaned and scored
600ml chicken stock
200g Spanish rice
50g snow peas
salt
1 bunch chives, chopped
1 lemon, cut into wedges, to serve

SOFRITO

2 large ripe tomatoes, roughly chopped
2 large roasted red capsicums from jar (piquillo)
4 cloves garlic, peeled
½ bunch parsley
½ bunch chives
25ml extra virgin olive oil
1 tsp saffron threads
1 tbsp smoked paprika

To make the sofrito, place all ingredients in a food processor and process until chunky. If you don't have a food processor then simply roughly chop the tomatoes and capsicums and finely chop the garlic and parsley and combine with other sofrito ingredients.

Heat a 30cm frying pan or paella pan on high heat, add chicken and seafood and cook until golden brown. Add sofrito and cook until tomatoes start to become juicy, 3–4 minutes. Add hot chicken stock and bring to the boil for 2 minutes. Stir in rice and bring to a simmer. Continue simmering for about 18 minutes.

When the rice is cooked and the liquid has almost fully reduced (there should still be some liquid in the fry-pan), add the snowpeas and cook for a further 2 minutes to achieve soccarrada (crust on the bottom of the pan)!

Season to taste with salt and garnish with chives. Squeeze over lemon juice just before serving.

HIGHER PROTEIN • SOFTER OPTION

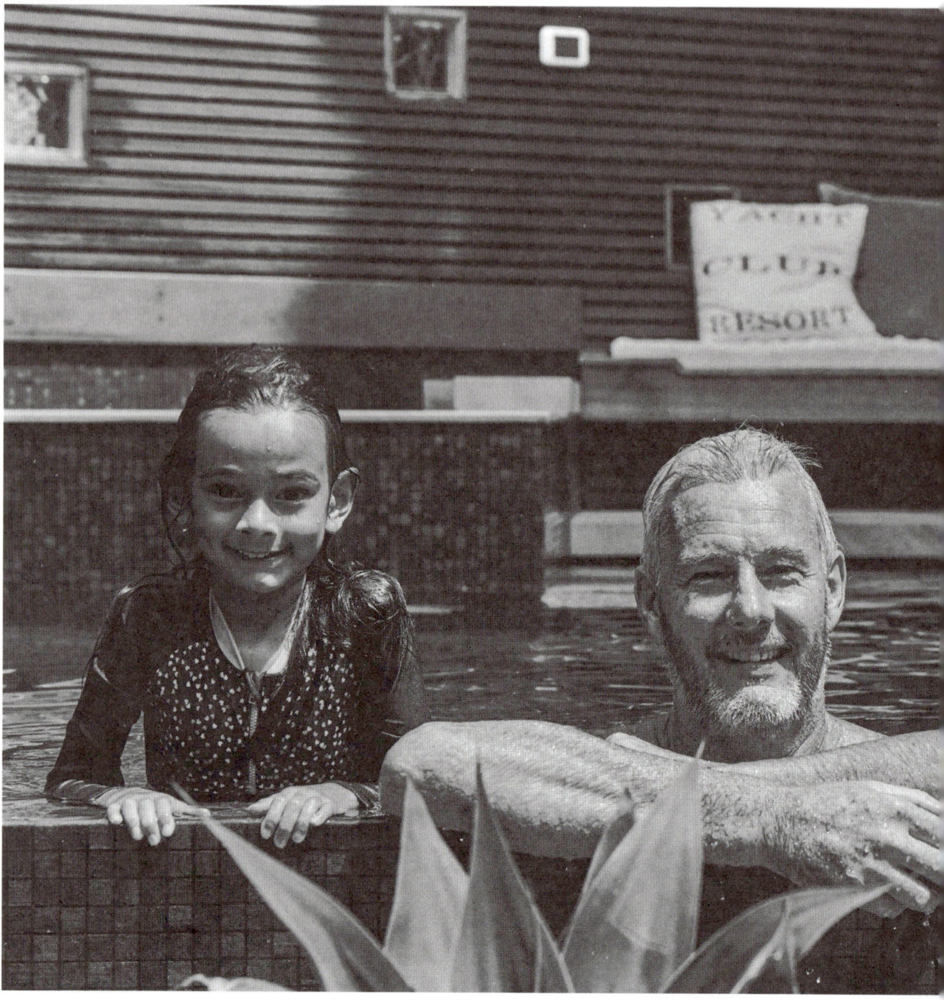
CLUB
RESORT

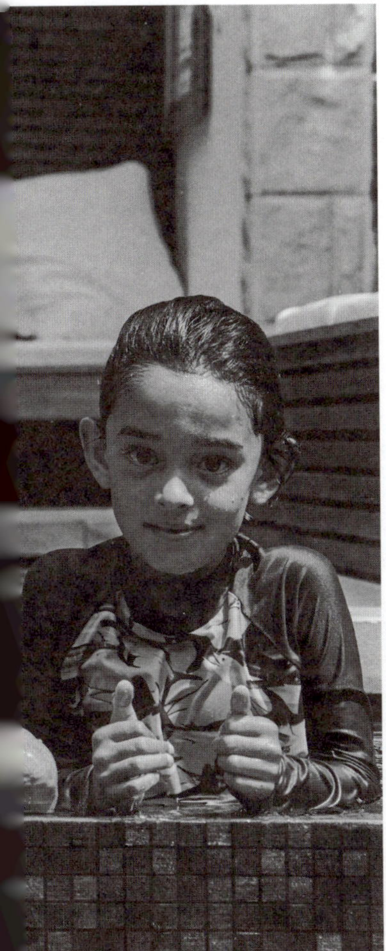

LIFE FORCE

DELICIOUS BARBECUED GARLIC CHICKEN WITH CAULIFLOWER AND BROCCOLI TABOULI

Most Australians love a good barbecue, or 'barbie', and we also love chicken and veggies. This recipe uses a lot of herbs instead of spices to make the chicken really tasty. The secret to keeping the chicken succulent and moist is to cook it only on one side, so the breast side does not touch the grill and the big garlic flavour is preserved. If you don't wanna butterfly the chicken, you could always ask your butcher to do it for you. Make sure you serve this dish on a big board, it looks a million dollars with the chicken resting on top of the tabouli.

Serves 6

1 large whole chicken

GARLIC MARINADE
1 head of garlic, cloves separated and peeled
¼ cup extra virgin olive oil
½ bunch lemon thyme
½ bunch thyme, leaves picked
½ bunch sage, leaves picked
2 sprigs rosemary
2 sprigs of oregano
generous pinch of sea salt flakes

TABOULI SALAD
1½ cups of cooked couscous
1 small head of cauliflower, grated (approx 500g)
½ small head of broccoli, grated (approx 300g)
½ punnet (125g) cherry tomatoes, quartered
½ small Spanish onion, diced
1 small zucchini, diced
1 medium bulb fennel, thinly sliced
1 bunch of parsley, finely chopped
1 bunch of coriander, finely chopped
1 bunch of basil, finely chopped
⅓ cup of extra virgin olive oil

>

Preheat your barbecue to maximum heat.

Grind the garlic in a mortar and pestle, gradually adding the olive oil until a paste is formed.

Add the herbs to the mortar and pestle and continue to grind until the mixture resembles a garlic butter. (You can do this stage in a blender)

Feel free to use any woody herbs you have handy – you want these hardier herbs as they will hold up better to the heat of the barbecue.

Next, spatchcock the chicken. Place the chicken breast-side down, with the legs towards you.

Using kitchen scissors or poultry shears, cut along each side of the parson's nose and backbone to remove it, cutting through the rib bones as you go.

Open the chicken out and turn over. Flatten the breastbone with the heel of your hand so that the meat is all one thickness. Alternatively you can use your knife to cut the sternum so that the bird lies flat.

Place the bird bone-side down on a chopping board. Using a chef's knife, score the chicken all over with deep cuts. This will help the flavour infuse into the meat and help the chicken cook quicker.

Rub the garlic marinade on top of the chicken and into the incisions.

Place the chicken bone-side down on the preheated barbecue, turning the heat down to medium high. Season well with salt. There is no need to flip the

HIGHER PROTEIN • HIGHER FIBRE

juice of 1 lemon
salt & pepper
1 tbsp sumac

TO SERVE (OPTIONAL)
½ cup Greek yoghurt
sprinkle of sumac

chicken, as the barbecue will steam the top until it is cooked through. Not putting the garlic marinade directly on the hot plate will also prevent it from burning and having a bitter taste.

Cover the barbecue and leave the chicken to cook for around 1 hour and 10 minutes.

Meanwhile, start preparing the salad.

To make the salad, mix the herbs and vegetables together in a large bowl. Dress with olive oil, lemon juice and spices and combine well.

Once the chicken is cooked through and the meat starts to come away from the bone, remove from the barbecue and cut into pieces.

Serve with Greek yoghurt, sumac and tabouli on the side.

LIFE FORCE

CARROT CAKE

When cooking, the best reward is seeing the little reactions of people just before they taste the food that you have cooked for them. This is the real meaning, the real pay-off. Bring carrot cake (or banana bread) just freshly made from home and you'll see smiles on people's faces ... and then a cup of tea ... and then a conversation ... and then – boom! – a connection, a little hope on a dark day, a little light in the tunnel. Roasting the carrots is a special process I like to do and is not very traditional but brings a natural sweetness to the cake that is special.

HIGHER PROTEIN • HIGHER FIBRE • LOW SPICE

Makes 10 slices

CAKE

500g medium carrots, roughly chopped into 3cm pieces
1 bunch of small heirloom carrots, top 1 cm greens cut off, cleaned and reserved
1 vanilla pod, split lengthways
2 tbsp vegetable oil
25g butter, cubed
4 eggs
1 cup walnuts
3 tbsp honey
2 tbsp peanut butter
1½ cups plain flour
2 tsp baking powder
2 tsp mixed spice
150g raw grated purple carrots
1 medium, raw grated beetroot

ICING

150g cream cheese, softened
50g butter, softened and cubed
zest of 1 lemon
2 tbsp vanilla essence or liquid stevia
1 tbsp maple syrup
1 tsp lemon juice

GARNISH

reserved carrot tops
1 tbsp poppyseeds
4 tbsp puffed quinoa

Preheat the oven to 180°C. Toss all the carrots in the vegetable oil and roast with the vanilla pod. Remove the heirloom carrots after 35-40 minutes, or when cooked through. Set aside. Discard the vanilla pod.

Cook the medium carrots for another 20 minutes or until cooked through and blistered. Remove and reduce oven to 160°C.

Blend the medium carrots and vegetable oil from the tray together with the butter, peanut butter, honey and eggs to form a smooth paste.

Add the walnuts and blitz briefly to keep the nuts in rough chunks.

In a separate bowl combine the plain flour, baking powder and mixed spice.

Gently fold the paste through the dry ingredients until a smooth batter is formed.

Fold the grated carrots and beetroot through the batter, set the heirloom carrots in the base of the cake and pour batter into a lined 20cm round springform cake tin, smoothing the top.

Bake for 45 minutes at 160°C or until just cooked when tested with a skewer. Allow the cake to cool in the tin.

For the icing, use an electric beater to combine the ingredients until light and fluffy.

Once the cake has cooled, carefully remove from the tin and peel away the baking paper.

Spread the icing generously over the top of the carrot cake, dot the carrot tops upright on top of the icing, sprinkle the top of the cake with the poppy seeds and quinoa puffs.

BANANA AND MANGO CHOC BLOCK

When Bazza told me how dehydrated he became in the process of his treatment, it made me remember how much Baz loves icy poles. So here we have two great cool ways to get flavoursome easy icy poles.

The key to get the stick right in the middle is using a little foil and don't get too caught up in the shape, just use containers that you have at home already like a little cup or a baking mould. Don't go and buy new ones – they always get lost in the cupboard anyway.

Makes 6

2 ripe mangoes, peeled and roughly chopped
2½ ripe bananas, peeled and roughly chopped
1 cup Greek yoghurt
foil wrap
pop sticks
200g milk chocolate, melted
1 cup shredded coconut

Blend mango, banana and yoghurt together until smooth.

Pour an even amount of mixture into 6 moulds, top with foil, insert a pop stick and freeze overnight if possible or until ready to eat.

Once frozen and ready to eat, remove the iceblock from the mould and dip in melted, cooled chocolate and roll in shredded coconut. Eat immediately.

COCO BERRY BARRY ICE BLOCK

Makes 4

strawberries, hulled and sliced
raspberries
blueberries
approx 2 cups coconut water
foil wrap
pop sticks

Fill moulds with equal quantities of sliced strawberries, blueberries and raspberries.

Top with coconut water, tapping the mould to ensure all air pockets are filled with liquid.

Top with foil, insert pop stick and freeze overnight if possible or until ready to eat.

LIFE FORCE

BANANA BREAD

Overripe bananas are the key to the best tasting banana bread. They will be easier to mash, sweeter and more flavoursome. Because they have so much natural sweetness, you can use more bananas, and less sugar.

Makes 10 slices

250g plain flour
2 tbsp baking powder
95g walnuts, roughly chopped
½ tsp cinnamon powder
6 ripe bananas, mashed
120g unsalted butter, softened
2 eggs, separated
1½ tbsp maple syrup

Preheat the oven to 175°C. Grease and flour an 11cm loaf tin.

Sift the flour and baking powder into a large bowl. Add the walnuts and cinnamon and stir until evenly combined.

In another bowl mash the ripe bananas until smooth. Add the softened butter, leaving small visible bits in the mixture. Add the two egg yolks and maple syrup and mix until smooth.

Add the dry ingredients into the wet ingredients.

Take the two egg whites and beat to form medium-soft peaks. Fold gently into the banana batter.

Pour the batter into the prepared loaf tin.

Top with the sliced banana and drizzle with the additional maple syrup. Bake for 60 minutes, or until a skewer inserted into the middle of the cake comes out clean.

Note: Overripe bananas are the key to the best tasting banana bread. They will be easier to mash, sweeter and more flavoursome. Because they have so much natural sweetness, you can use more bananas, and less sugar.

SOFTER OPTION • LOW SPICE

AVOCADO MOUSSE

Avocado is frequently used in South American cuisine for pastry and a never-ending list of desserts; it is creamy and very smooth. This recipe is moreish and once you've had the first mouthful you won't be able to stop until it is finished! The difference between the smooth texture of avocado mousse and the crunch of the nuts is pure … satisfaction.

Serves 6

1 lime, zested and segmented, segments set aside for garnish
wedge of lime
20g pecans
20g walnuts
20g pistachios
2 ripe Shepard avocados
360g cream cheese
5 limes, juiced
4 tbsp maple syrup
handful of blueberries and raspberries for garnish
mint leaves, optional garnish

Place the lime zest into a shallow bowl. Moisten the rim of 4 balloon glasses using the lime wedge. Holding each glass upside down, dip the rim into the lime zest so it sticks. Set remaining zest mixture aside for garnish.

Place pecans, walnuts and pistachios in a ziplock bag and crush to large crumbs using a rolling pin. Evenly distribute the crushed mixture into the base of the 4 glasses. Keep a small amount aside for garnish.

Remove avocado from skins using a large serving spoon, being sure to scrape as close to the skin as possible as this is where all the flavour is. Reserve 2 tablespoons of avocado to use for garnish, diced.

Mash the avocado, cream cheese and lime juice together using a fork or stick blender. When smooth, add maple syrup and whip with a whisk to combine and add air.

Spoon the mixture evenly into the 4 glasses, and smooth over the crumble base.

Cut the reserved avocado into 1cm cubes. Garnish the 4 glasses with the reserved diced avocado, lime zest, reserved crumb mixture, berries and small mint leaves (optional).

HIGHER PROTEIN • SOFTER OPTION • LOW SPICE

LIFE FORCE

BARRY DU BOIS & MIGUEL MAESTRE

ALMOND AND BLUEBERRY TART

My mum have done the famous Camino of Santiago where this tarts are served to get some energy along the hundreds of kilometers than the pilgrims walk to clean their souls, almonds are soooo full of goodness and they are delicious the blueberries is a personal touch as is not very traditional Spanish but a total signature ingredient in Australia and as well full of the good stuff

I guess I choose this recipe one of my signature dishes as going through the journey of cancer is pretty much like a very long Camino and along the way we can get nurtured not just with food but with the support of our family and friends

Bazz always tells me than everyone's support has been one of the key ingredients to make him feel better in the harder moments

Makes 10 slices

PASTRY
250g plain flour
20g icing sugar
125g cold butter, chopped
3 egg yolks
pinch of salt

FILLING
125g unsalted butter
25g caster sugar
2 eggs
100g almond meal
1 tsp plain flour
finely grated rind of 1 orange
finely grated rind of 1 lemon
75g chocolate chips

TOPPING
4 tbsp double cream
3 punnets blueberries

Preheat oven to 175°C.

Grease a 24cm round, loose based fluted cake tin.

Sift flour and icing sugar into a processor. Add the butter and process until crumbly. Add yolks and salt and process until ingredients just come together. Wrap dough in plastic wrap. Refrigerate for an hour.

Roll dough between two sheets of baking paper until large enough to line prepared tin. Lift dough into tin and press it into sides. Refrigerate for 15 minutes.

Line the prepared dough with baking paper. Fill with rice or baking beans to stop it rising. Cook in the oven for 10 minutes. Remove the paper and weights. Return to oven for a further 3 minutes or until the tart shell is dry and lightly browned. Cool.

To make the filling, beat the butter and sugar in a small bowl with an electric mixer until light and creamy. Add the eggs one at a time, beating between additions. Stir in the almond meal, flour, rind and chocolate chips. Spoon the filling into the tart shell.

Cook in the oven for 30–35 minutes or until the tip of a knife comes out clean when inserted. Cool completely.

To serve, spread the double cream on top of the tart and then arrange the blueberries on top, covering the tart completely with blueberries.

HIGHER PROTEIN • LOW SPICE

LIFE FORCE

RICE PUDDING

Try to define the meaning of comfort food and rice pudding would be the first one in the dictionary
Is a gentle, filling and warm dessert that would slow down the world while you eating it, rice is one of Spanish favourite ingredient and it works as well in sweet than savoury.

My best memories of yummy desserts are full with rice pudding and the smell of cinamon and vanilla all over the house.

Serves 6

2 oranges, rind and segments
2 lemons, rind and segments
1L milk
200g Spanish rice
4 tbsp honey
2 vanilla beans, split, seeds scraped out
1 cinnamon quill
75ml cream

Rinse a medium heavy based saucepan with cold water but don't dry it. Add milk and rice to pan. Bring to a boil over medium heat. Reduce heat. Stir in rind, honey, vanilla beans and seeds, cinnamon quill. Simmer, stirring occasionally, for about 30 minutes or until pudding is thick and creamy and rice is tender. Remove from heat. Stir in cream. Remove vanilla beans and cinnamon.

Divide mixture among four flameproof ramekins, 13cm round x 3cm deep.

Serve with orange and lemon segments.

HIGHER PROTEIN • SOFTER OPTION • LOW SPICE

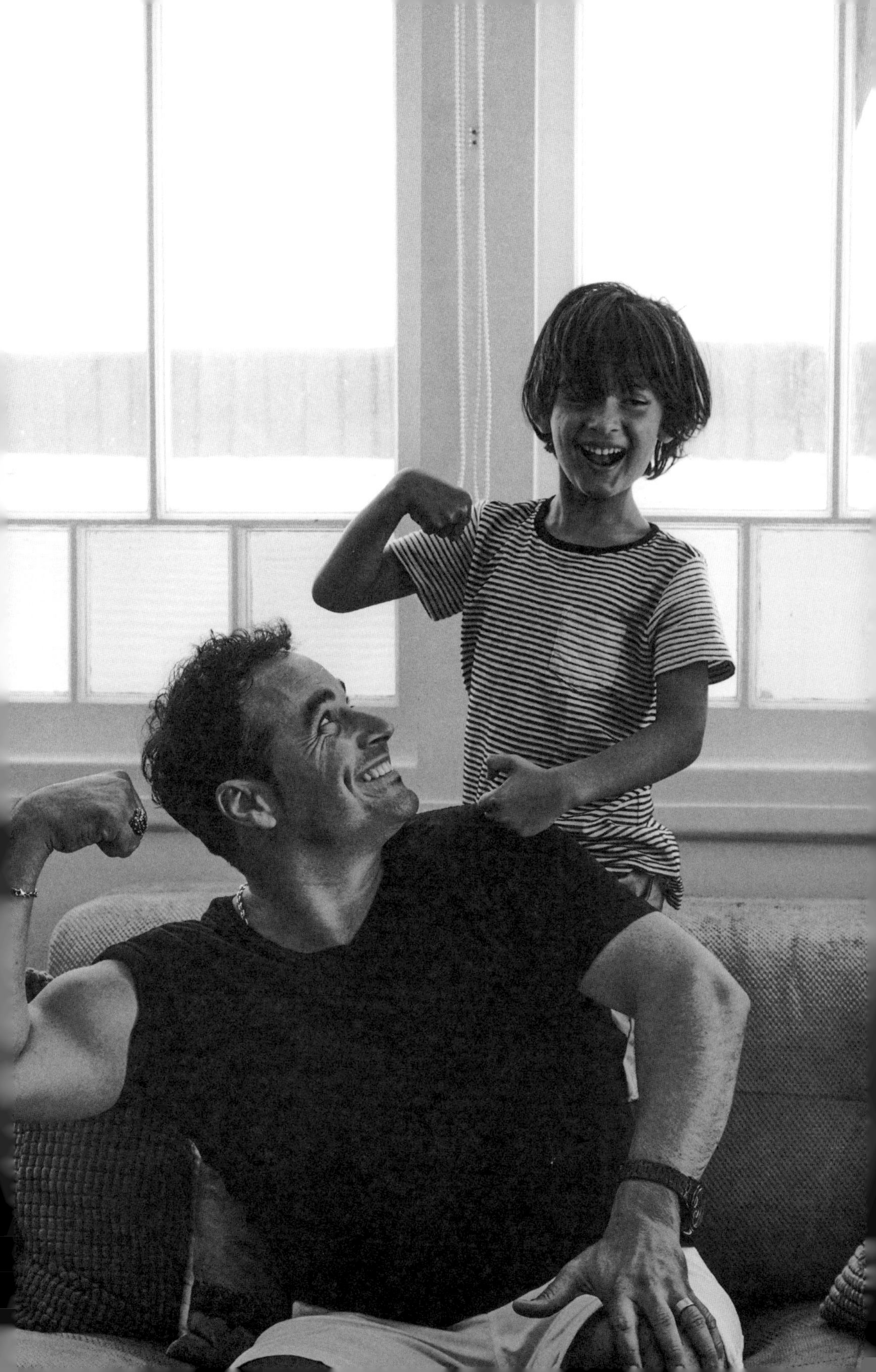

LIFE FORCE

BARRY'S SPECIAL THANKS TO
Dr Sam Milliken and the nurses and staff at The Kinghorn Cancer Centre, St Vincent's Hospital, Sydney. Dr Judith Lacey and the staff at Chris O'Brien Lifehouse Comprehensive Cancer Hospital. My brother and sister, Liz and Mick, and my friends who have lived every second of my life with me. Derek Rielly, for the therapeutic mid-morning chats and who helped me create this book. Amanda, Chris and Miguel for their support and belief in me and the thousands of beautiful people who have allowed the four of us into their homes each week. The love and support you've given to me is a huge part of this fight.

To those who have shared with me their challenges with cancer and depression, thank you. You're an inspiration.

MIGUEL'S SPECIAL THANKS
Firstly, I want to thank my beautiful wife Sascha for all the support she gives me every single day. She is also the best mummy to Claudia and Morgan. You keep me grounded. You're my rock, TE QUIERO! I would also like to thank my princess Claudia and superhero Morgan. You're the spark of my fire every day when I get up to go to work. A massive thank you to my papa Antonio and my mama Florentina. You are the best mum and dad anyone could ask for.

A massive thank you to our amazing TV family – Barry, Chris and Amanda. You are the truest of friends, and always there for me no matter how far away you are, or how late it is. We have a real chemistry and connect in a supernatural way.

To my dear friend and agent Tracy Gualano. Thank you for organising my life, and the never-ending list of emails, recipes and calls every day. I know that cancer is also close to your heart, and your papa will be very proud of you.

I'd also love to thank Derek. You are so great at what you do. I am honoured that you accepted this project and turned it into the most beautiful story. A storyteller like no other.

A massive thank you as well to Bazza's super wife of the millennium, Leonie. I know the amazing support you give to Barry, and how much he loves you. You are truly inspirational, and a fantastic cook!

And finally, thanks to Chris O'Brien Lifehouse Comprehensive Cancer Hospital for doing such a great job, and being such a unique organisation. To Judith and Merran, thank you for all our chats about nutrition. Your knowledge and passion to help people feel better is contagious.